THE GARDEN LOVER'S GUIDE TO
Germany

THE GARDEN LOVER'S GUIDE TO

Germany

CHARLES QUEST-RITSON

PRINCETON ARCHITECTURAL PRESS

First published in the United States in 1998 by
Princeton Architectural Press
37 East 7th Street
New York, NY 10003
212.995.9620

For a free catalog of other books published by Princeton Architectural Press,
call toll free 1.800.722.6657 or visit www.papress.com

First published in Great Britain in 1998 by Mitchell Beazley, an imprint
of Reed Consumer Books Limited, London

Library of Congress Cataloging-in-Publication Data for this title is
available upon request from the publisher.

ISBN 1-56898-131-7

For Mitchell Beazley
Executive Editor: Guy Croton
Executive Art Editor: Ruth Hope
Editor: Selina Mumford
Designer: Terry Hirst
Editorial Assistant: Anna Nicholas
Illustrator: Paul Guest
Cartographer: Kevin Jones
Picture Researcher: Anna Kobryn
Production: Rachel Staveley

For Princeton Architectural Press
Project Coordinator: Mark Lamster
Cover Design: Sara E. Stemen
Special thanks: Eugenia Bell, Caroline Green, Clare Jacobson, Therese Kelly,
and Annie Nitschke – Kevin C. Lippert, *publisher.*

Half title page: Schloss Eremitage, Bayreuth
Title: Arboretum, Eberswalde
Contents: Killesberg Park, Stuttgart

Printed in Singapore

02 01 00 99 98 5 4 3 2 1 First Edition

Contents

How to use this book

This guide is intended for travellers who wish to visit the most historic and beautiful gardens of Germany. The book is divided into three chapters covering the major regions. Each chapter comprises an introductory section with a regional map and a list of the gardens, followed by entries on each garden. The entries are accompanied by detailed at-a-glance information telling the reader about the garden's defining characteristics and nearby sights of interest. The guide also includes five "feature" gardens, specially illustrated by three-dimensional plans.

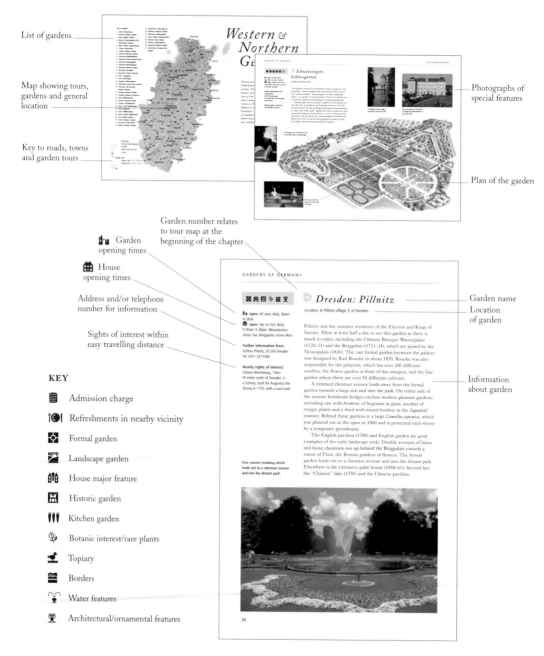

List of gardens

Map showing tours, gardens and general location

Key to roads, towns and garden tours

Photographs of special features

Plan of the garden

Garden number relates to tour map at the beginning of the chapter

🏵 Garden opening times

🏠 House opening times

Address and/or telephone number for information

Sights of interest within easy travelling distance

Garden name

Location of garden

Information about garden

KEY

🏧 Admission charge

🍽 Refreshments in nearby vicinity

✿ Formal garden

🏞 Landscape garden

🏠 House major feature

🏛 Historic garden

🌾 Kitchen garden

🌱 Botanic interest/rare plants

🌳 Topiary

🌿 Borders

💧 Water features

🏺 Architectural/ornamental features

Foreword

I visited over 200 gardens when writing this guide, from
Flensberg to Konstanz and from Trier to Frankfurt-an-
der-Oder. It was hard to make my selection of 114 for this
book. They had to be representative while also including
every top-class botanic, historic or civic garden. Among
the wonderful gardens that I regret being unable to include
are Schloss Moritzburg near Dresden, Schloss Fasanerie
near Fulda and Schloss Fantaisie near Bayreuth, as well as
the botanic gardens at Hof, Siegen and Giessen. Other
factors I considered were their state and condition, and
how often they are open to the public. Few private gardens
are open often enough to merit inclusion. Insel Mainau is
a conspicuous exception and, with two million visitors
each year, is one of the world's most popular gardens.

Almost all of Germany's best gardens are open early
every day and free of payment. The German people are
helpful, friendly and hospitable, and English is widely
spoken. But do not assume that grass is for walking on. It
is always better to start from the premise that everything
is *Verboten* unless expressly permitted.

Late summer bedding in
Berlin's Tierpark.

Introduction

Germany has wonderful historic gardens, great botanic gardens and inspirational modern ones. Each, in its way, is as good as its equivalent in other countries. My advice is to go and see them for yourself. Germany is indeed a garden-lover's paradise.

This book will help you to plan your visits. You will soon discover that there is a sharp divide, for example, between historic gardens and those of more horticultural or botanic nature. Historic gardens seldom have any features other than the historic. There was, however, such a flowering of gardens throughout the 18th and 19th centuries, that both the Baroque and the landscape traditions are very well represented in Germany.

The great historic gardens come in geographical clusters. Each is associated with the culture of one of the great German princes. They therefore tend to be close to historic cities and not, as in other countries, in remote country areas. It is useful to understand something of Germany's history – the horrors of the Seven Years War,

Parkland and azaleas: the Schlossgarten at Oldenburg.

Napoleon's destruction of the temporal bishops and why the Elector Carl Theodor of the Palatinate suddenly became King of Bavaria. To understand fully Germany's historic gardens it is important to appreciate both the political and social aspirations of the garden makers. The great landscape garden at Wörlitz is an expression of Prince Franz's commitment to the principles of the Enlightenment.

The Germans' scholarship and energy are seen at their best in historic gardens, which are forever being restored, replanted, redesigned or expanded. Some that were remade after the Second World War have now been restored for the second or third time. This means that some best features may be out-of-bounds for many months: there is nothing to do but return later for the parts that you could not see on your first visit. And the Germans love adding unhistorical embellishments. They commemorated the 1972 Olympics in Munich by inserting a Japanese garden in the middle of the Englischergarten (see p.77), one of the world's greatest 18th-century landscape parks. Question their sense of historical appropriateness, and they are quick to justify themselves: such additions are most instructive, therefore they are good.

It is scarcely surprising that the English landscape movement found sympathy among the German people. A love of nature runs deep in the German soul. This movement developed new forms of compelling beauty in Germany long after the English had forgotten it. What you do not get in Germany, however, is the plantsmanship of English and American gardens, founded on the acquisitiveness of garden owners and a fashion for planting for colour effects. Germany has the New Planting instead, developed by the Potsdam nurseryman

The garden of summer annuals at Dresden Botanic Garden.

Potsdam's Botanic Garden is among the best maintained.

Karl Förster and his disciples in the early years of this century. It involves planting large quantities of mainly herbaceous plants in an apparently random arrangement which allows the plants to grow, spread and self-seed in imitation of a natural distribution. But the New Planting is not the only fashion which is currently enjoying a good run. Many modern German gardens also take inspiration from Japanese precedents, as well as from American modernism.

Visitors cannot fail to be struck by the number and excellence of German botanic gardens and their glasshouse collections. Most have adapted well to illustrate the modern orthodoxy of biodiversity. The Germans are also good at habitat collections, particularly of their local flora. Visitors are not kept away from the working areas of botanic gardens but can usually inspect such parts as the frames where young plants are growing on. Keen plantsmen will come across many plants in German botanic gardens that are new to them and return home with long lists of species and varieties that they wish to grow for themselves.

The private gardens of Germany which are open to the public are few and disappointing. German garden owners tend not to express their creative individuality in the garden. Gardening is generally regarded as a civic or corporate activity, and best undertaken by a botanical institute or a government ministry. No other country can boast such magnificent civic gardens – often developed with federal money for the biennial Bundesgartenschau – as Grugapark in Essen (see p.116) and Dortmund's Westfalenpark (see p.113). They combine exciting modern designs with spectacular horticultural effects, and botanical seriousness with a sense of public amenity. Together with Germany's great historic and botanic gardens, they are immensely rewarding to visit.

The autumn colour of the maples in Bielefeld's Botanic Garden.

Key to gardens

1 Berlin: **Arboretum Späth**
2 Berlin: **Botanic Garden**
3 Berlin: **Charlottenburg**
4· Berlin: **Klein-Glienicke**
5 Berlin: **Pfaueninsel**
6 Berlin: **Tiergarten**
7 Cottbus: **Branitz**
8 Dessau: **Georgium**
9 Dessau: **Luisium**
10 Dessau: **Mosigkau**
11 Dessau: **Oranienbaum**
12 Dessau: **Wörlitz**
13 Dresden: **Botanic Garden**
14 Dresden: **Grosser Garten**
15 Dresden: **Gross-Sedlitz**
16 Dresden: **Pillnitz**
17 Eberswalde: **Arboretum**
18 Gotha: **Schlosspark**
19 Greifswald: **Botanic Garden**

20 Jena: **Botanic Garden**
21 Leipzig: **Botanic Garden**
22 Ludswigslust: **Schlosspark**
23 Muskau: **Schlosspark**
24 Neuruppin: **Temple Garden**
25 Neustrelitz: **Schlosspark**
26 Oberhof: **Rennsteig Garden**
27 Potsdam: **Babelsberg**
28 Potsdam: **Neuer Garten**
29 Potsdam: **Sanssouci**
30 Rheinsberg: **Schlosspark**
31 Sangerhausen: **Rosarium**
32 Schwerin: **Schlossgarten**
33 Weimar: **Belvedere**
34 Weimar: **Park an der Ilm**
35 Weimar: **Tiefurt**

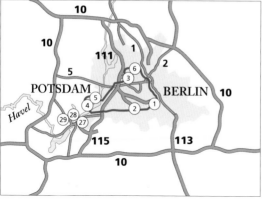

The gardens to be seen in
Berlin and Potsdam.

Key

===== Motorways
===== Principal trunk highways
(3) Gardens
⬤ Major towns and cities
● Towns

Garden tours

—— Dessau tour: 8, 9, 12, 11, 10
—— Berlin tour: 1, 2, 4, 5, 3, 6

Eastern Germany

Map labels:

Stralsund

Greifswald (19)

109

96

Anklam

w

Alten-treptow

enburg

Pasewalk

198

96

litz (25)

Prenzlau

irg • Füstenberg (30)

11

uppin

167

Eberswalde (17)

ERLIN

Frankfurt

12

102

Luckenwalde

87 Beeskow

stadt berg

101

Lübbenau

15

187

87

COTTBUS (7)

Elster-werda

Bad Muskau (23)

Elbe

4

Görlitz

6

14

Meiben (13)(16)

4

(14)(15) DRESDEN

170

CHEMNIZT

174

95

Treble

The gardens of eastern Germany are distinctly different from those in the rest of the country. It was here that the landscape movement took root and where the lurch to neoclassicism was first seen during the 19th century. The Baroque is less in evidence, though Gross-Sedlitz near Dresden (see p.33) is an under-appreciated masterpiece and Frederick the Great of Prussia, who was still making Baroque gardens when everyone else had switched to landscapes, had surprisingly conservative tastes. But the thin sandy soil of Prussia, with its cool lakes and dark forests, has bred a taste for restraint in architecture and landscaping. Only in the fertile hills of Saxony can the first hints of exuberance and enjoyment be seen.

Eastern Germany is the best place to see the work of all the most significant landscapers. Indeed one of the great excitements of German reunification (in 1990) has been the opening up of the whole world of German landscaping. The German landscape movement was a development of the English. Travellers in the 18th and 19th centuries visited Britain to observe, study, and learn. Then they returned home to interpret what they had seen in a German context. Prince Franz of Anhalt-Dessau designed his

13

Rosa 'Futtaker Schlingrose' in Sangerhausen's Rosarium.

This jolly 19th-century statue of a 16th-century buccaneer is at the Temple Garden at Neuruppin.

mega-landscape at Wörlitz (see pp.28–31) in homage to the parks he had seen in England at Claremont, Stourhead, and Stowe. He extended his landscaping from one end of his principality to the other: it is still known as the Gartenreich. Goethe was fired by Wörlitz to landscape the Park an der Ilm at Weimar (see p.54) and he in turn inspired the roistering Prince Hermann von Pückler-Muskau (Prince Pückler) best known for his work at the gardens of Babelsberg (see p.44), Branitz (see pp.22–3) and the Schlosspark in Muskau (see pp.40–1). He was followed by Eduard Petzold and such prolific designers as Peter Joseph Lenné, who thus constitute an apostolic succession of landscapers from the first practitioners until the end of the 19th century.

Once the Germans adopted the natural English landscape, they never reacted against it. Apart from Lenné's exquisite Sicilian Garden at Sanssouci (see p.48), the Italianate gardens of Victorian England have no comparable manifestation anywhere in Germany. Protestant Prussia had a flirtation with neoclassicism in the 19th century, when the architect and town planner Karl Schinkel designed landscapes and garden buildings in and around Potsdam, as well as the public buildings which contribute greatly to the beauty of Unter den Linden, the grandest street in Germany. However throughout eastern Germany parks and gardens were laid out in the English landscape style until the middle of the 20th century.

Most botanic gardens in the ex-DDR (German Democratic Republic) show the effect of intellectual and financial impoverishment under Communist rule. Many appear to be old-fashioned, under-funded and badly maintained when compared to those in the West. They still reflect the priorities of fifty years ago: biodiversity and conservation are not yet the driving orthodoxies. Their visitor guides tend to be written in a style which, rather than inspiring and informing visitors, lectures them on the general principles of botany and reveals little of what to expect in the garden. The gardens, however, remain in the traditional hearts of their university cities, instead of being banished to a soulless new site on the outskirts, as so often in the West. The inner city position of the greatest gardens, Leipzig and Jena (see pp.37–8), are one of their charms. You should, however, consider how they would have developed if they had been in West

Berlin's Charlottenburg garden was restored during the 1950s as a pastiche.

Germany. Some are already changing – for example the Rosarium at Sangerhausen (see p.51) and the Rennsteig Garden at Oberhof (see p.43) have each emerged as successful tourist attractions – unthinkable in the 1980s.

The truth is that there are still two Germanies. To a foreign visitor, the differences between the *Länder* of the East and the West are still very noticeable. Motorists should remember that roads are rougher in the East and travel much slower. Long diversions, unexplained queues, and immovable traffic jams are an everyday occurrence. Visitors will find much that is run down and inefficient in the ex-DDR. Standards of maintenance are often disappointing and there is an inefficiency about the way some gardens are managed in the East.

Nevertheless, for some of the greatest historic gardens, there is nothing to compare with the best that eastern Germany can offer: Wörlitz near Dessau and, above all, Sanssouci at Potsdam. It is here that we see the genius of Lenné at its most dazzling: the expansive landscape around the Havel is breathtaking both for its beauty and its scale. There is much to be learned, too, from the lesser-known parks of Dessau, which are as undervisited as the great Wörlitz is busy. A visit to the gardens of Dresden teaches us the power and riches of the Saxon court. The substantial gardens of Mecklenburg-Pommern in Schwerin, Neustrelitz, and Ludwigslust make one wonder that anything so grand could come from such an impoverished region. For that is the real wonder about eastern Germany: how a region so lacking natural resources and deficient in industry can have dominated the whole of Germany for so long and so successfully, not just in the greatness of the gardens and landscapes, but in the world of political and military endeavour.

Part of the glasshouse range at the Berlin Botanic Garden.

🛢 🖼 🏛 ⚘

open: Apr to Oct, Wed to Sun
and Public Holidays, 10am–6pm

Further information from:
Späthsches Arboretum,
Späthstrasse 80/81, 12437-Berlin
Tel: 0306 366941

Nearby sights of interest:
Treptower Park.

Conifers frame this glade in
the arboretum.

Berlin: Arboretum Späth

Location: At the junction of Späthstrasse and Britzerallee

Franz Späth laid out this 3.5ha (8.6 acre) arboretum in the 1870s,
to the designs of Gustav Meyer. It served as a private garden, a
dendrological testing ground and a showplace for customers of
the nursery. Meyer designed the arboretum in the English style,
with winding paths leading through closely planted spaces and
wide open glades in other areas.

Today the arboretum is a wonderful collection of mature trees
and shrubs of horticultural and botanical interest: some 1,200
taxa represented by 5,000 plants. Among the most handsome of
the older, centennial trees are *Quercus alba* f. *elongata* and *Aesculus
hippocastanum* 'Umbraculiferum'. Other trees worth looking out
for are the seldom-seen *Fagus sylvatica* 'Striata' and a female form
of *Ginkgo biloba* which fruits regularly. All the plants are named,
as in a botanic garden, which adds enormously to the value of
a visit. A rock garden was added in 1931, in a natural style in
keeping with the rest of the garden. *Juniperus* x *pfitzeriana* is a
living holotype – the original parent plant of all the millions now
in cultivation. The arboretum is well maintained: its gravel paths
are raked, even in the most remote corners.

🍴 🏛 🍴 ⚘ 🍽

open: Daily at 9am. Closes
at 3pm in Mar; 4pm from Nov to
Feb; 5pm in Oct; 7pm in Apr and
Sep; 8pm from May to Aug.
The glasshouses are open at 9am
(10am on Sat, Sun and Public
Holidays) and close at 3.15pm
from Nov to Feb; 4.15pm in Mar
and Oct; 5.15pm from Apr to Sep.
The Botanic Museum is open all
year, Tue to Sun, 10am–5pm

Further information from:
Botanischer Garten, Königin-
Luise-Strasse 6–8, 14195-Berlin
Tel: 030 830060

Nearby sights of interest:
Dahlem museum complex.

Berlin: Botanic Garden

Location: Entrances in Unter den Eichen and from Königin-Luise-Platz

This is one of the world's leading botanic gardens and worth a
long visit at any time of the year. It has fine living collections
backed by all the infrastructure needed for tourism and amenity.
It was founded in 1679 but moved to its 48ha (119 acre) site at
Dahlem about 100 years ago. The 14ha (35 acre) arboretum is
arranged according to plant families. The geographical displays
and the chain of rock gardens are the best in the world.

More than half the garden's 18,000 taxa are in the glasshouses.
These include palm houses, orchid collections, a "Victoriahaus"
for tropical waterlilies, Bromeliaceae, rhododendrons and
camellias, economic plants, cactus houses for succulents, and a
carnivorous plant house. An opulent bedding scheme runs down
in front of the glasshouses, where displays of tender plants are
put out for the summer. There are extensive habitat plantings,
including a water garden, a moorland garden, an Italian Garden,
a scented garden, and a rose garden. Berlin's Botanic Garden
attracts many visitors but, even on the busiest day, you can
always find peace and solitude in the remoter parts of it.

Berlin: Charlottenburg

Location: In the centre of Charlottenburg

The formal garden at Schloss Charlottenburg was created in 1697 for Kurfürstin Sophie Charlotte, by Siméon Godeau (a pupil of André Le Nôtre), and extended in 1705. It was the first French Baroque garden in Germany. Purists claim that nothing remains of the original garden: it was unhistorically restored in the 1950s and is now but a scanty pastiche. The truth is that the Baroque ground plan is still recognizable: the large formal garden is edged by pleached trees and extended by a long formal lake at the end. Its parterres are of gravel and grass, somewhat patchily planted with teucrium, and along the sides rich seasonal bedding reaches its peak in early autumn.

The Baroque shapes were landscaped away, first by Johann August Eyserbeck in 1788 and later by Peter Joseph Lenné. The original geometrical lake was softened in 1802, but the cast iron bridge at the end of the lake, which dates from 1799, has not been altered. Beyond it is an English park, somewhat informally maintained. The Belvedere (1788) originally stood on an island in another lake. At the furthest end is an obelisk (1979). To one side is the Mausoleum, with a circle of rhododendrons in front and an avenue of yews and firs leading up to it: all evergreen, solemn and sombre. The Schloss has been stunningly restored, and its paintings, furniture, and porcelain are well worth seeing.

open: All year, daily, 6am–8pm

open: All year, Tue to Fri, 9am–5pm; Sat and Sun, 10am–5pm; closed Mon

Further information from:
Schloss Charlottenburg,
Luisenplatz, 10585-Berlin
Tel: 030 320911

Nearby sights of interest:
Agyptisches Museum.

Schloss Charlottenburg has been entirely rebuilt since 1945.

Berlin: Klein-Glienicke

Location: By Glienicke Bridge, which connects Berlin and Potsdam

open: All year, daily, daylight hours

Further information from:
Schloss Klein-Glienicke,
Königstrasse, 14163-Berlin

Nearby sights of interest:
Pfaueninsel; Babelsberg; trips
on the Havel; all the sights
of Potsdam.

Klein-Glienicke is an integral part of the Potsdam landscape. Its views and sight-lines connect with Babelsberg (see p.44), Pfaueninsel (see opposite), the Marmorpalais Palace, and other major buildings around the edge of the Havel lakes. Peter Joseph Lenné first laid out its pleasure grounds for Prince Hardenberg in 1816, but continued to work there for Prince Carl of Prussia (one of Frederick William IV's brothers) after Hardenberg's death in 1822: the two royal princes had just returned from a tour of Italy with a collection of archaeological spoils. Some of these are incorporated in the Kleine Neugierde, a neoclassical temple inset with genuine Greek and Roman wall paintings, inscriptions, reliefs, and mosaics. Nearby is an arrangement of fallen columns which originally came from Cap Sunion. The surrounding grounds are beautifully landscaped with fine copper beeches, planes, and lime trees. Steps lead up from the lakeside to the Casino, a neoclassical villa, which Karl Schinkel built in 1824. Neat classical colonnades stretch out on either side.

The Schloss is an elegant neoclassical building, attached to an Italianate conservatory and a cloister which contains much of Prince Carl's archaeological collection. Schinkel's Lion Fountain is the best-known feature of the garden: a pair of golden lions, high on two colonnaded plinths, spew jets of water into a pool below. In 1840, Ludwig Persius designed the nearby Roman-style Stibadium, with a granite basin in front. Along the Havel edge are the powerhouse, boathouse, viewpoint, and the Devil's Bridge, built as if an artificial waterfall had partly destroyed it. There is a Tudor-Gothic Jaegerhof right at the end of the park.

Antique ruins from Cap Sunion at Klein-Glienicke.

Berlin: Pfaueninsel

Location: Ferry from Nikolskoer Weg

The magic island of Pfaueninsel is part of the overall landscaping which Peter Joseph Lenné designed for Potsdam and the Havel in the first half of the 19th century. Its conspicuous, white folly of a "ruined" castle is from an earlier period and was built in 1796 for Frederick William II's mistress Gräfin Lichtenau. Frederick William II commissioned the building of the Meierei (the Gothic ruin at the northernmost end of Pfaueninsel) and the neoclassical Jacobsbrunnen with its broken Corinthian columns. It was Frederick William III who allowed Lenné to landscape the whole island. He also collected botanical rarities, so that to this day Pfaueninsel is worth visiting for its unusual trees, some of which are over 200 years old.

The small and pretty Round Garden near the house was originally laid out in 1821 around a pergola of robinia trunks clad with different ornamental climbers. It is planted with bedding, carefully worked for colour and height, with lots of plumbago in summer. Below it is a rose garden, restored as it was originally in 1821, with old varieties, many grown as standards, planted in long narrow beds. The rest of the island is given over to classical landscaping and, of course, to the peacocks which give the island its name.

A stately grassy drive runs from the castle to the Meierei at the far end of the island. The woodland is mainly of oak, but there are glades of meadow flowers rich in natural species. Other excitements include a Doric portal (brought from Charlottenburg, see p.19) known as the Luisentempel, with a bust of Queen Luise of Prussia inside, a house clad in bark, an aviary in the woods, a small lake, a handsome iron fountain on the highest point of the island, some gothic stables designed by Karl Schinkel (their façade came from a medieval house in Danzig), and a Gothic cast iron bridge. Pfaueninsel is the most enchanted and peaceful landscape in Berlin: some would say in the whole of Germany.

open: Daily, May to Aug, 8am–8pm; Apr and Sep, 8am–6pm; Mar to Oct, 9am–5pm; Nov to Feb, 10am–4pm
open: May to Oct, Tue to Sun, 10am–5pm (closes 4pm in Oct)

Further information from:
Pfaueninsel in der Havel, Berlin
Tel: 030 8053042

Nearby sights of interest:
Schloss Klein-Glienicke.

This cast iron fountain is high in the woodland at Pfaueninsel.

open: All year, daily, dawn to dusk

Further information from:
Tiergarten, Strasse des 17 Juni, 10623-Berlin

Nearby sights of interest:
Brandenburger Tor.

Water, trees, and spacious parkland are the essence of Berlin's Tiergarten.

Berlin: Tiergarten

Location: Between Stadt Mitte and Charlottenburg

It is the sheer size of Berlin's Tiergarten that most impresses the visitor, as well as its plum position, right at the heart of the city, linking the neoclassical quarter, the Unter den Linden, with Charlottenburg (see p.19). The main road, Strasse des 17 Juni, runs straight through the Tiergarten's middle, but the magnificent gilded Angel of Victory stands so tall in the centre of the park that it can be seen from every corner and serves to unify its 220ha (544 acres).

The Tiergarten is made up of dense deciduous woodland, underplanted in parts with rhododendrons, azaleas and other ornamental shrubs, and punctuated by lakes, open spaces, and special horticultural or historical features. Its present ground-plan owes most to Peter Joseph Lenné, who reworked the Tiergarten in the 1830s, but it was utterly destroyed during the battle for Berlin (1945) and has been restored and replanted since the war.

The greatest pleasure of the Tiergarten is to walk its long, shady avenues and enjoy its stately peacefulness. But there are many fine features to admire, and even a minimalist tour should take in the following: the Englischer Garten, the Königin Luise Denkmal, the Rosengarten, and the Rousseau Insel. Of these, the Rosengarten is outstanding: a formal enclosure, apparently cut out of the woodland, centred on a granite Italianate fountain with a statue of Flora, the Roman goddess of flowers, at one end. Roses of every kind are extravagantly planted with a rich mixture of herbaceous perennials and annuals chosen to create a sense of opulence. The memorial to the much-loved Queen stands on a small island, and the surrounding lakeside is vividly planted with spring bulbs and summer bedding.

open: All year, daily, dawn to dusk
open: All year, Tue to Sun, 10am–6pm (closes 5pm from Nov to Mar)

Further information from:
Park Branitz, 03042-Cottbus
Tel: 0355 751 521

Nearby sights of interest:
Old buildings in Cottbus.

 # Cottbus: Branitz

Location: On the south-eastern outskirts of Cottbus

After Prince Pückler had to sell the Schlosspark at Muskau (see pp.40–41) in 1846 he retired to Branitz and immediately set about improving its landscape. Two lakes and the pleasure ground were completed within the first five years: other features included the Blauer Garten, the Rosenhügel, the Kiosk, and a bust of the singer Henriette Sonntag in a gilded arcade. Some of the existing farm buildings were demolished, and others were given a Tudor-Gothic facing. The house was remodelled by Gottfried Semper who also built the pergola or "Italian wall" to

display Prince Pückler's collection of terracotta reliefs and
bronzes by the famous Danish sculptor Bertel Thorwaldsen.

Three main rides open out in front of the Schloss, helped by
the undulations introduced by Prince Pückler to add movement
to the flat site. After his wife's death in 1853, Prince Pückler
extended the park to the west by 50ha (124 acres) and began to
build earth pyramids or "tumuli". His first pyramid, in one of the
lakes, was finished in 1856: it contains the grave of Prince
Pückler and his wife, which is inscribed with the words "Graves
are the mountains of a distant new world". This pyramid bursts
into flame in early autumn when the Virginia creeper covering it
turns to scarlet and crimson. In 1863 the "land" pyramid was
built, and several years later alterations were made to the
Serpent Lake. Work had already began on the Hermannsberg
(a third pyramid) when Prince Pückler died in 1871. His nephew
inherited the estate and added the final touches to the
Hermannsberg, the Schlangensee and the Westpark, until his
uncle's plans were finally completed in 1888. Branitz had then
attained its present size of 160ha (395 acres) and the Pücklers
had planted more than 250,000 trees, mainly oak, beech, lime,
hornbeam, and maple. Allow plenty of time for a visit, as there is
much ground to cover in this complex, carefully designed and yet
so natural-looking landscape garden.

Each of the bridges was
individually designed and named.

Dessau: Georgium

Location: On the NW side of the town

open: All year, daily, dawn to dusk

open: All year, Tue to Sun, 10am–5pm

Further information from:
Park Georgium, 06813-Dessau
Tel: Dessau tourist office
0340 214661

Nearby sights of interest:
Bauhaus architecture and the Bauhaus Museum.

This extensive garden was landscaped by Prince Franz of Anhalt-Dessau, with help from his gardener J Eyserbeck. It is named after the Prince's younger brother Johann Georg, to whom he gave it in 1779. Originally there were many more buildings and ornamental incidents within the park's 60ha (148 acres), but time and conflict have much reduced their number. What remains is unfortunately in a bad state of repair at present. Indeed, the park is so overgrown in parts that it is once again inhabited by deer.

The palace has a simple white façade, anglo-Tuscan in outline. It was built by von Erdmannsdorf in 1780 and is complemented by formal gardens. To the right is an Ionic temple, known as the Blumengartenhaus, with a pretty display of bedding plants in front. On the other side are the remains of another Ionic temple, which once housed the kitchens for the Schloss: it was destroyed in 1945 and has not yet been repaired.

The Schloss enjoys a grand view sideways towards the Monopteros temple, a little Ionic cupola with ten white columns. Nearby are some "Roman" ruins based on the seven pillars of the Temple of Saturn in the Roman Forum, Italy. A wide variety of long views run through and across the landscape but many are obscured by overgrowth and undergrowth. In the woodland are a ruined bridge, statues of the Dying Cleopatra and the Sleeping Hermaphrodite. Right at the end of the garden, the Wallwitz Castle looks out towards the River Elbe, and the Elbe pavilion itself overlooks an ancient dock on the edge of the river.

The "ruined" bridge has recently been "restored".

Dessau: Luisium

Location: Badly signposted: 2km (1¼ miles) NW of Dessau, beyond the village of Waldersee

Luisium is the most intimate of the landscapes of Dessau: this intimacy derives from its human scale and the harmony between its monuments and their setting. Its 14ha (35 acres) were laid out from 1774 onwards by J F Eyserbeck as a summer residence for Princess Luise von Anhalt-Dessau, wife of the great landscaper Prince Franz. The park itself is a beautiful classical composition of glades and groves (mainly of oak, hornbeam, lime and beech) with long vistas into the Elbe meadows. It is entirely enclosed by a raised dyke which, as well as supplying protection from flooding, offers a magnificent vantage point for viewing the park, its buildings, and the landscape outside. Walking along the dyke reveals the geometry of the garden and its long axial views: the main features appear and reappear as one walks around.

open: All year, daily, dawn to dusk

Further information from:
Park Luisium, 06831-Dessau
Tel: Dessau tourist office
0340 214661

Nearby sights of interest:
Park Georgium.

The Schlangenhaus was based on Eton's Gothic buildings.

The Landhaus is small, white and pretty – taller than it is long or wide – and perched on a small mound above the long lake in the west of the park. Near to the Landhaus a stepped Chinese bridge leads to a classical gardenhouse, once surrounded by flower beds, and to a small grotto and fountain. A long view runs down from the building towards a distant pyramid attached to the tower of the parish church in the nearby village of Jönitz. Another axis connects the early 18th-century Gothic pavilion, known as the Schlangenhaus, with a stud farm in the Elbe meadows which has been given a Gothic façade. Other pretty incidents include the Orangery, two neo-Gothic gatehouses by the east entrance, and a picturesque ruin, with Corinthian pilasters, after a model in the ancient city of Palmyra.

10 *Dessau: Mosigkau*

Location: In the centre of the village, SW of Dessau

open: All year, daily, dawn to dusk
open: Tue to Fri: May to Sep, 10am–6pm; Apr and Oct, 10am–5pm; Nov to Mar, 10am–4.30pm; Sat and Sun, 11am–4pm; closes Mon. Guided tours only

Further information from:
Tel: 0340 214661 (Dessau tourist office)

Nearby sights of interest:
The Dessau Gartenreich.

Exotic tender plants in Versailles cases line the courtyard behind the Schloss.

The best view of this garden is from the entrance gates to the south, through which a short, broad drive runs between low box hedges towards the elegant Schloss. Unfortunately, however, the main entrance for visitors is now from Knobelsdorffallee, to the side of the Schloss, and leads into the *cour d'honneur* behind. The original Rococo garden was laid out from 1752 to 1757 for Anna Wilhelmine, Princess of Anhalt-Dessau. It was redesigned in the landscape style in the 19th century, but the principal axis was preserved and some of the original statues still line the drive today. The lawns on either side are planted with fine old trees, including copper beeches and American oaks. Two 18th-century orangeries, near the south gates, house some ancient plants, including a 200-year-old pomegranate. Many pots of lemons, bay trees, agaves, and dasylirions are put out in front of the Schloss for the summer, while oleanders and daturas in white-painted Versailles cases are positioned around the lawns.

In front of the Schloss is a small *parterre de broderie* with attractive summer bedding. Near the south-eastern corner of the garden is a goldfish pond with taxodiums upon its banks. Opposite is a hornbeam maze and, beyond it, a Japanese garden, presided over by a rustic summerhouse called the Chinese house (1774), which is decorated with imitation palm trunks. *Maackia chinensis* trees add to the oriental effect when they flower in late summer. Modern sculptures around the grounds, are, perhaps, a little out of harmony with the classical beauty of the garden.

Dessau: Oranienbaum

Location: In the centre of the village, 10km (6 miles) from Dessau

The formal garden was first laid out by Cornelis Ryckwaert in 1683 for Henriette Catherina of Nassau-Oranien, the wife of Prince Johann Georg von Anhalt-Dessau. Nothing remains of the once extensive parterre, except an expanse of grass and a little bedding around the central fountain. Tubs of agapanthus and tender plants are put out along the edges of the grass during the summer months. The formal garden was once flanked on one side by a maze, now a young coniferous plantation. The nearby orangery (1812–18) is the third to be built on the site but all its orange trees were killed by frost c1960.

Beyond the parterre was the formal Baroque park, now very overgrown, though the main ride through the woods is lined with naturalized rhododendrons and azaleas and makes a magnificent sight when they are in full flower. On the other side of the parterre was an island garden formed by diverting a stream. Franz von Anhalt-Dessau redesigned it in 1795 as a Chinese garden, and there is a magnificent tea-house on the edge of a lake strewn with rocky islets, several small Chinese bridges, and a five-storey pagoda modelled on the one designed by William Chambers at Kew Gardens, near London.

This was the first Chinese landscape garden in Germany and remains the most extensive. It has been restored several times but is still close to the original design.

open: All year, daily, dawn to dusk

open: Check with tourist office. The pagoda is open May to Sep, Sat and Sun, 2–4pm

Further information from:
Schlosspark, 06785-Oranienbaum
Tel: 0349 422033 (Tourist Office)

Nearby sights of interest:
The village of Oranienbaum.

The Chinese house at Oranienbaum is set among winding rocky islets.

Dessau: Wörlitz

Location: In the village of Wörlitz: well-signposted

open: All year, daily, dawn to dusk

open: Apr and Oct, Mon, 1–4.30pm; Tue to Sun, 10am–4.30pm. May to Sep, Mon, 1–6pm; Tue to Sun, 10am–6pm. Guided tours only

Further information from:
Schloss und Park Wörlitz, 06786-Dessau
Tel: 034905 20216 and 21704 (Dessau tourist office)

Nearby sights of interest:
Oranienbaum.

Wörlitz is the most important landscape garden in Germany – breathtakingly beautiful and blessed with an apparently endless number of delightful features. It was laid out from 1768 to 1800 by Prince Franz von Anhalt-Dessau who adopted the progressive agricultural, industrial, and social reforms of contemporary England. Naturally he was also influenced by the writer and philosopher Rousseau, the embodiment of the Enlightenment, and by the great classicist Winckelmann. He travelled widely in England and often copied such gardens as Stourhead, Stowe, and Claremont. A considerable Italian influence is also detectable in the New Gardens.

Prince Franz sought both to beautify the landscape and to improve his estates. Wörlitz extends to about 120ha (300 acres), of which some 80ha (200 acres) are lakes and agricultural areas which have been worked into the parkland. The lakes were

Venus bathing near the principal ferry station.

The elegant Chinese bridge has a very wide span.

The parkland merges into the natural landscape.

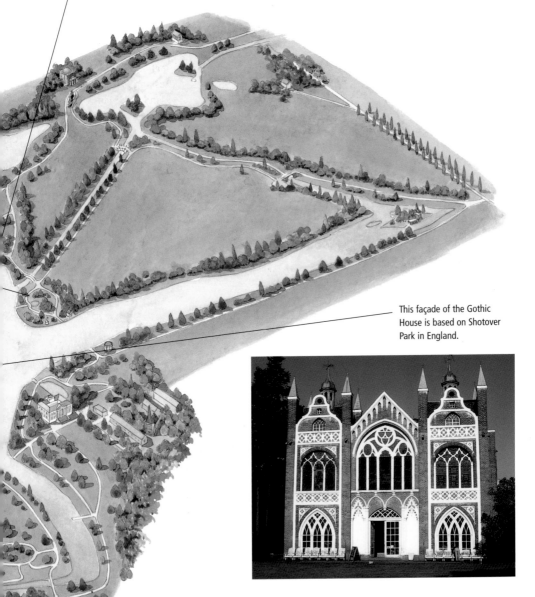

This façade of the Gothic House is based on Shotover Park in England.

formed as a result of floodwater breaching the embankments of the Elbe. The whole park was designed as a complex system of spatial relationships, with sight-lines (short and long), and groups of trees planted in the landscape style. Architecture, landscaping, and painting all contribute to the whole. Seats, monuments, and paths have each been positioned with a deliberate effect in mind, to offer the greatest variety of mood and impressions during a tour. There are fine individual trees, pretty spring bulbs and excellent rhododendrons, and other items of horticultural interest, but all are secondary to the park.

Prince Franz rebuilt the Schloss or Landhaus between 1769 and 1771 according to a Palladian design by James Gibbs in *A Book of Architecture* (1728). To one side of the Schloss is the Englischergartensitz, a charming summerhouse modelled on one at Stourhead, Wiltshire: it is one of the earliest Palladian garden buildings in Germany. Other interesting features in this part of the garden include the Marstall, which was given a neo-Gothic façade between 1775 and 1776, and the substantial Synagogue built between 1787 and 1790 to resemble the Temple of the Vestal Virgins in Rome. Neumark's Garden, named after one of the Prince's gardeners, Johann Christian Neumark, is a gondola ride away across an arm of the Wörlitzer lake. The outstanding features here are the Labyrinth and an area known as Elysium, both built between 1783 and 1784 as allegories of the life of man. The nearby Rousseau Island is identical to the one at Ermenonville, north of Paris: an urn sits on a short pedestal surrounded by dignified Lombardy poplars.

It is only a short gondola ride from this part of the garden to the Rose Island and across to Schoch's Garden, so-called after another of Prince Franz's gardeners, Schoch the elder. Pause on the Wolf Bridge and look down the canal towards the Temple of Venus (1794), which is a copy of Colin Campbell's Temple of Venus at Hall Barn, Buckinghamshire. It looks wonderful when framed by *Rhododendron ponticum* in early summer. The Gothic House (1773), whose southern façade is based on Shotover Park, Oxfordshire, was the first Gothic revival building outside Britain. Even prettier is the northern façade in the ornate Gothic *gotico fiorito* style of the Madonna dell'Orto in Venice. Behind the Gothic House a short avenue frames the Temple of Flora (1797–98), which is a copy of the original at Stourhead. Nearby is the elegant curving wooden White Bridge over the Wolf Canal, which resembles Sir William Chambers' Chinese bridge at Kew Gardens, near London.

The Kettenbrücke appears as a chainbridge attached to a romantically ruined tower.

Other charming features in this part of the garden include the
Golden Urn and the ruin attached to the Kettenbrücke, a wood-
en bridge on a chain. Seen from the High Bridge, some 100m
(328ft) away, it resembles a rope bridge.

The Weidenheger is a comparatively undeveloped part of
the garden that has been embellished with such statues as the
Boy with a Thorn and Venus Bathing. On the edge of the New
Gardens, the most Italian part of Wörlitz, there is also a
roothouse and an Iron Bridge (1791) which was copied from
the revolutionary iron bridge in Shropshire, near the English
border with Wales. The most interesting monuments here
are a scale copy of the Pantheon (1795–97) and the Stein, an
imitation of the volcano at Vesuvius which was ignited by a
great fire that spewed forth ashes, smoke and flames. Red-tinted
glass portholes found in the sides of the 25m (82ft) cone were
illuminated from inside. Water was then pumped over the lip
of the cone so that it would flow down the outside in
imitation of molten lava.

Wörlitz's gardens have no boundaries and are accessible to
everyone. They became very overgrown during the communist
era but have since been restored. All visitors should ponder the
inscription on the Warnungsaltar: "Wandere, achte Natur und
Kunst und schone ihrer Werke" ("Passer-by, have respect for
Nature and Art, and value their works").

Early autumn colours on part
of the lake known as the
"Kleines Walloch".

The "Hohe Brücke" ("High
Bridge") on the edge of the lake.

Dresden: Botanic Garden

Location: NW corner of Grosser Garten (see below)

open: Daily: Apr to Sep, 8am–6pm; Mar and Oct, 10am–5pm; Feb and Nov, 10am–4pm; Jan and Dec, 10am–3.30pm

Further information from:
Botanischer Garten, Dresden, Stübelallee 2, 01307 Dresden
Tel: 0351 4593185

Nearby sights of interest:
Grosser Garten.

This botanic garden was founded in 1820 but moved here, to the north-west corner of the Grosser Garten (see below), in 1893, only to be utterly destroyed by enemy bombing in 1945. The garden's 3.5ha (8.6 acres) contain some 9,000 taxa. Botany is well served by the collections of North American plants, plants from Saxony and Thüringen, medicinal and culinary herbs in a modern physic garden, and a small collection of bog plants. There is also a substantial rock garden that concentrates upon European plants from the Pyrenees to the Caucasus, as well as the Alps. But the outstanding feature is a handsome and extensive display garden of annuals and vegetables: some 800 different taxa are grown from seed every year, so that local people can learn what will grow in their own gardens.

Tender exotics are well catered for in a range of glasshouses, which include a cactus house, an orchid and carnivorous plant house, a "Victoriahaus", and a big tropical house. The whole garden is maintained to a high standard: one senses that the gardeners are fully in control.

Dresden: Grosser Garten

Location: Just to the SE of the city centre

open: All year, daily, dawn to dusk

Further information from:
Grosser Garten, 01069-Dresden

Nearby sights of interest:
Dresden Botanic Garden.

The ruined palace is reflected in the vast formal water tank at the centre of the Grosser Garten.

The Grosser Garten is a huge English-style park, some 141ha (348 acres) in extent. It was once the great garden of the Electors and Kings of Saxony. Four avenues of lime trees lead up to the handsome palace, which was built at the end of the 17th century. The long lateral Herkulesallee and the Südallee were originally laid out in 1683, but were replanted following the devastation of 1945. In front of the palace is a long formal water tank with a tall single jet playing in the middle. It is hedged with hornbeam and flanked by six pretty yellow-painted garden pavilions.

The remoter parts of the park were first laid out as formal woodland with star-shaped rides for hunting, but these were simplified in the landscape style. In 1950 the Grosser Garten was restored as a Socialist Peoples' Cultural Park. It was spruced up with children's playgrounds, sports grounds, a pioneer railway, and an open air theatre. Relics of this régime include a dahlia trials garden, banks of rhododendrons chosen to show what can survive the cold winters of Saxony, and trials of such herbaceous plants as phlox. The summer bedding is excellent, but the Grosser Garten is a pleasure to visit in every season.

Dresden: Gross-Sedlitz

Location: In the village of Heidenau

open: Daily: Apr to Sep,
7am–8pm; Oct to Mar, 8am–6pm

Further information from:
Barockpark Gross-Sedlitz
Tel: 03529 519212

Nearby sights of interest:
The countryside to the south and
east of Gross-Sedlitz, known as
the Saxon Switzerland.

This is one of the great Baroque gardens of Europe: all the more pity, therefore, that it should be so little known. Gross-Sedlitz is a series of huge compositions: formal set pieces which lead the eye across the Elbe valley and on to the Sandstein Hills. The garden was begun in 1719 by Count Wackerbart, but most of it was made by King Augustus the Strong after 1723.

The entrance is down a double staircase above a bowling green but, having arrived there, it is by no means clear where the visitor should turn next. Walk to the far side and onto the roof of the Lower Orangery (originally built by King Augustus but altered in the 1860s), above the magnificent semicircular orangery parterre, and look across to a grand double staircase at the far end, known as the Stille Musik because of its statues of musician-cherubs. Further along on the right is the Upper Parterre, which is flanked on one side by the Upper Orangery and on the other by Friedrichsschösschen. The main view from the Friedrichsschösschen is to the Upper Parterre, down the bowling green and over a ha-ha at the end. The cross-axis from the Upper Orangery runs across the Upper Parterre and over the Water Parterre to a wonderful Baroque cascade running through woodland. All the main features are tricked out with balustrading, vases, urns, and numerous 18th-century statues.

The Orangery Parterre at Gross-Sedlitz is a masterpiece of the Baroque.

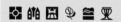

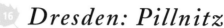

Dresden: Pillnitz

Location: In Pillnitz village, E of Dresden

open: All year, daily, dawn to dusk

open: Apr to Oct, daily, 9.30am–5.30pm. Wasserpalais closes Tue; Bergpalais closes Mon

Further information from:
Schloss Pillnitz, 01326-Dresden
Tel: 0351 2613260

Nearby sights of interest:
Schloss Moritzburg, 15km (9 miles) north of Dresden, is a Schloss, built for Augustus the Strong in 1720, with a vast park.

Pillnitz was the summer residence of the Electors and Kings of Saxony. Allow at least half a day to see this garden as there is much to enjoy, including the Chinese Baroque Wasserpalais (1720–21) and the Bergpalais (1723–24), which are joined by the Neuespalais (1826). The vast formal garden between the palaces was designed by Karl Bouche in about 1870. Bouche was also responsible for the pinetum, which has over 200 different conifers, the flower garden in front of the orangery, and the lilac garden where there are over 50 different cultivars.

A trimmed chestnut avenue leads away from the formal garden towards a large urn and into the park. On either side of the avenue hornbeam hedges enclose modern pleasure gardens, including one with *broderies* of begonias in grass, another of steppe plants and a third with mixed borders in the *Jugendstil* manner. Behind these gardens is a large *Camellia japonica*, which was planted out in the open in 1860 and is protected each winter by a temporary greenhouse.

The English pavilion (1780) and English garden are good examples of the early landscape style. Double avenues of limes and horse chestnuts run up behind the Bergpalais towards a statue of Flora, the Roman goddess of flowers. The formal garden leads out to a chestnut avenue and into the distant park. Elsewhere is the extensive palm house (1858–61): beyond lies the "Chinese" lake (1791) and the Chinese pavilion.

Fine summer bedding which leads out to a chestnut avenue and into the distant park.

Eberswalde: Arboretum

Location: Signposted, S of Eberswalde, off the road to Melchow

This important arboretum was founded in 1830, which makes it one of the oldest in Germany, and its scientific work has greatly benefitted the whole country. It has two parts: 20ha (49 acres) for experimental forestry and 8ha (20 acres) for ornamental trees, each grounded in the inevitable sandy soil of Prussia. Important timber trees, like European larch from known provenances, are trialled in established blocks and compared for their disease resistance, growth, hardiness and ornamental value.

The ornamental part of the arboretum has over 1,100 taxa. The collection is arranged to some extent geographically and planted with trees of all ages: some impressive old oaks give structure to much younger plantings. Among the many handsome specimen trees are the American hazel *Corylus americana*, the huge-leaved *Tilia x moltkei*, *Liquidamber styraciflua*, which is magnificent in the autumn, and the rare Andalusian pine *Abies pinsapo*. Ornamental underplantings have made it a woodland garden which is particularly attractive in early summer when the rhododendrons and azaleas bloom, and the meadows are purple with wild *Geranium palustre*. An excellent collection of willows (notably *Salix nigricans* and *S. eleagnos*) and alders surrounds a lake, fringed by mare's tail 2m (6½ft) high. A small rock garden is charmingly planted with edelweiss, campanulas, dianthus and *Primula farinosa* and there are systematic beds for herbaceous plants, as well as a small display of tropical plants in summer. For dendrologists it is a place to study and reflect.

open: All year, daily, dawn to dusk

Further information from:
Forstbotanischesgarten der Institut für Forstwissenschaften, 16225-Eberswalde-Finow

Nearby sights of interest:
The gigantic barge-lift (Schiffshebewerk) at Niederfinow on the Havel-Oder canal.

Horticultural cultivars in the 19th-century arboretum at Eberswalde.

Gotha: Schlosspark

Location: In the town centre

The Schlosspark at Gotha is large, and dominates the centre of the town although unfortunately it is cut by two roads, Parkallee and Friedrichstrasse. Schloss Friedenstein is a huge rectangular building at the top, but there is a formal garden with bright bedding in front of Schloss Friedrichstal to the east. This is all that remains of a much larger Baroque garden which survived until the earliest years of this century. The area between Schloss Friedenstein and the Museum of Nature is now dominated by a modern memorial to the victims of fascism.

The large English-style park to the south of the museum is one of the earliest landscapes in Germany, and was first laid out in 1766 by Duke Ernst II of Saxe-Gotha-Altenburg, who later

open: All year, daily, dawn to dusk
open: All year, Tue to Sun, 9am–5pm

Further information from:
Schlosspark, 99867-Gotha

Nearby sights of interest:
The historic buildings in Eisenach and the Wartburg, some 30km (19 miles) west of Gotha.

added the Doric Temple as a place of contemplation: two of his sons who died in infancy are buried on the island in the lake below. In the parkland there are some good clumps of trees, mainly beeches, whose size and position indicate the original layout, somewhat obscured by modern plantings.

Goethe wrote enthusiastically of the park after a visit in 1783. In 1845, however, Prince Pückler observed that parts of the park were poorly maintained. Unfortunately the garden is still in a sorry state, and Gotha needs to take responsibility for the upkeep and restoration of its garden heritage.

open: All year, daily, 9am–6pm

Further information from:
Ernst-Moritz-Arndt-Universität
Arboretum Botanischergarten,
17489-Greifswald
Tel: 03834 861 136

Nearby sights of interest:
Greifswald's Gothic brick cathedral and magnificent bell tower.

19 *Greifswald: Botanic Garden*

Location: Off Wolgaster-Strasse, at the junction of Billroth-Strasse and Friedrich-Ludwig-Jahn-Strasse; not signposted

The arboretum at Greifswald was begun in 1934 and now extends to 8ha (20 acres). The comprehensive collection is made up of some 1,400 taxa arranged geographically, so that the plants can be seen in their natural combinations. Conifers are a great feature of the garden, and lend mass to its structure: the site is flat and many of the raked gravel paths are straight, but the plantings create a sense of enclosure.

Among the most notable deciduous trees are fine individual specimens of *Gleditsia caspica* and *Juglans cinerea*, whose ferocious thorns, up to 30cm (12in) long, stick straight out of the trunk and the branches. The Birkenwald is a very pretty area planted with different birches, which are underplanted with a wide range of rhododendron species. Nearby is a heather garden interplanted with dwarf conifers and other members of the Ericaceae family, including both species and forms of *Arbutus*, *Enkianthus* and *Gaultheria*. The adjoining sunken fern garden is planted next to the pool whose sides have attractive herbaceous groupings of astilbes and hemerocallis. Additions are constantly being made to the collections.

This is a garden in which to wander gently and study. It is perhaps best visited in late spring when the rhododendrons are in full bloom, but it is interesting at any time of the year for visitors to discover what plants will grow in the sandy soil of a windswept Hansa port.

Greifswald also has a small botanic garden, in Münter Strasse just behind the railway station: its 16 greenhouses cover some 1,800 sq m (19,000 sq ft) and support everything from a cactus house to a "Victoriahaus". It also has an alpine garden, large areas of naturalized aconites, which flower in early spring, and a collection of medicinal plants.

These mature conifers give structure to the plantings at Greifswald.

Jena: Botanic Garden

Location: In the city centre

open: 15 May to 14 Sep, Tue to Sun, 9am–6pm; 15 Sep to 14 May, 9am–5pm. Glasshouses open at 10am in winter

Further information from:
Botanischer Garten,
Fürstengraben 26, 07743-Jena
Tel: 03641 8222208

Nearby sights of interest:
Inspektorenhaus Goethe
Gedenkstätte.

The garden started as a small *Hortus Medicus* in 1586, which makes it the second oldest botanic garden in Germany after Leipzig (see p.38). It has a major herbarium, with more than 2.6 million specimens. Goethe designed the Inspektorenhaus in 1827, which adjoins the garden on the south side. The garden extends to 4.5ha (11 acres), and has about 12,000 taxa, of which some 3,500 are in the alpine collection.

Jena is best known for its living collections of mountain and rock plants: the extensive rock gardens are magnificently constructed of different geological stones and are thickly planted. The habitat collections include woodland plants, steppe plants, moor plants, heath plants, and sand plants. The largest tree in the garden is a Hungarian oak, *Quercus frainetto*, and the oldest is a *Ginkgo biloba* planted in 1790.

The glasshouses were rebuilt between 1980 and 1983, and include a cactus and succulent house; a subtropical house, mainly for evergreen trees from rainforests; a subtropical house for water plants and marginals; a "Victoriahaus" for tropical water plants; and a fine palm house with more than 40 species of tropical palms. The wonderfully exotic courtyard garden between the greenhouses is decorated with interesting sculptures, as well as tender plants in summer. The garden as a whole is attractively landscaped and has begun to recover from communist neglect.

The courtyard, enclosed by the greenhouses, is home to an exotic collection of sculptures.

Leipzig: Botanic Garden

Location: Off Pragerstrasse, about 1km (½ mile) SE of the city centre

open: Daily: Apr to Sep, 9am–6pm; Oct to Mar, 9am–4pm. Glasshouses open weekdays, 1–4pm

Further information from:
Botanischer Garten der Universität Leipzig, Linnéstr. 1, 04103-Leipzig
Tel: 0341 9736850 and 9736851

Nearby sights of interest:
Old buildings in the Altstadt, including the Altes Rathaus and Alte Börse.

A bust of Linnaeus, the father of modern botany.

Leipzig's botanic garden was founded in 1542, which makes it the oldest in Germany. Originally a physic garden attached to the university, it has a distinguished history and many well-known botanists worked here. It was badly bombed during the war and much of its fabric is old and decaying, but it manages to cram some 8,000 taxa into its 2ha (5 acres), including many plants that are not widely available in cultivation.

The arboretum is laid out systematically, according to the plant orders: the Magnoliaceae section is particularly attractive in spring when the magnolias are in flower, but there are also fine specimens of the trees *Castanea mollissima, Pterocarya* x *rehderiana* and *Syringa reticulata* var. *amurensis*.

Many of the geographical beds too are dominated by woodland flora, notably those devoted to the Far East, the Rockies, and eastern North America. There are two systematic areas, one for monocotyledons (plants with one seed leaf) and the other for dicotyledons (plants with two seed leaves), both of which are large and full of interesting plants. These display gardens are dominated by hardy and half-hardy annuals, gourds, garden flowers, and herbs. Most of the rest of the garden is put to ecological collections, including plants from heathlands and sandy soils, chalk-lovers, moorland plants, and bog plants. There is a small rock garden and an attractive large area devoted to the steppe flowers of Europe and Asia.

The comprehensive range of glasshouses (somewhat rusty, old-fashioned and antiquated) has dedicated houses for palms, rainforest plants, tropical water plants (including the papyrus plant, *Cyperus papyrus*, both species of the giant amazonian waterlily and the sacred Indian lotus *Nelumbo nucifera*), the Cape flora, carnivorous plants, and subtropical evergreens. There is also a butterfly house, open for a short period in July and August. Leipzig's botanic garden has much to offer the visitor.

Ludswigslust: Schlosspark

Location: In the town centre

Duke Frederick of Mecklenburg-Schwerin adopted Ludwigslust as his new seat of government in 1764. South of the dilapidated Schloss is a magnificent cascade, beyond which a lime avenue leads to the town church. The cascade was originally made of wood, but refaced with sandstone in 1775. There are further waterworks in the Schlosspark, including a circular cascade with 24 fountains and a big canal. Nothing remains of the long parterre, now a lawn, north of the Schloss, but the view along the central axis is extended down the Hofdamenallee, a lime avenue through the woods.

On an island to the west of the Schloss is a Hansa-Gothic Catholic church, built in 1818, with a detached bell tower. Elsewhere are two mausoleums, a small ruin, and a Swiss Cottage, which is more of a princely residence than a folly.

The spacious Schlosspark on the north and west sides of the palace is laid out in the classical English landscape style. Peter Joseph Lenné was asked to redesign the landscape in 1852 and, although it has reverted to unmanaged woodland, the main vistas which he developed through the surrounding woods and meadows still exist, at least in outline. Many of the park's elements are still there, including handsome trees, extensive lakes, and banks of rhododendrons, but forty years of proletarian rule have destroyed much that is historic and beautiful.

open: All year, daily, dawn to dusk
open: All year, Tue to Sun, 10am–8pm (closes 5pm in winter)

Further information from:
Schlosspark, 19288-Ludwigslust
Tel: Ludwigslust tourist office
03874 29076

Nearby sights of interest:
The town church.

The waterfall in the main courtyard, south of the Schloss.

open: All year, daily, dawn to dusk

Location: In the town centre

Further information from:
Schlosspark, 02953-Bad Muskau

Nearby sights of interest:
Cross over into Poland and visit the rest of the park.

Muskau is the largest classical 19th-century landscape park ever made. Since 1945, however, the German-Polish frontier runs through the middle and now only 200ha (494 acres) are left in Germany: the remaining 350ha (865 acres) lie in Poland. Muskau was the birth-place of the swashbuckling German landscaper Prince Pückler. He began to lay out the park as a young man in 1815, buying whatever further land he could from the people of Muskau. He then made several journeys to England, where he was much influenced by the ideals of the famous landscaper Humphry Repton. Prince Pückler commissioned the painter Wilhelm Schirmer to draw parkland views which he then copied on the ground. Karl Schinkel drew up architectural plans too, but they were never executed.

These ornamental urns near the Schloss are still planted as Pückler intended.

In 1821 Prince Pückler constructed an artificial tributary of the Neisse, called the Hermannsneisse, which was channelled through the Schloss moat and then into a new lake called the Eichsee before re-entering the Neisse over a beautiful long cascade. But Prince Pückler's ideas were grandiose and

extravagant. He had little regard for the agricultural use of land or even the need for income. Landscaping was a work of art: it would create a social Utopia. Eventually Prince Pückler overspent, and was forced to sell up.

In 1846, Muskau was bought by Prince Frederick of the Netherlands, who rebuilt the Schloss in the Renaissance style. It was burnt down in 1945. The castle was connected to the park by an extensive pleasure ground and some areas of bedding remain as a link to the 19th century. Prince Frederick improved the park between 1852 and 1881, with the constant help of Eduard Petzold, and extended it yet further.

Today, Muskau is magnificent, mature parkland, and a great joy to walk through. Many of the trees are of stately size: specimens of plane, weeping beech, red beech, evergreen conifers and taxodiums with knobbly aerial roots. A clump of *Aesculus parviflora* is more than 30m (98ft) in diameter. The rhododendrons and azaleas are ravishing in spring.

Neuruppin: Temple Garden

Location: Close to the town centre

open: All year, daily, 9am–6pm

Further information from:
Tempelgarten (Amalthea Garten), 16816-Neuruppin

Nearby sights of interest:
The Heimatmuseum, Rheinsburg.

The Musentempel is one of Frederick the Great's earliest garden buildings.

This garden takes its name from the charming Musentempel, a Doric fantasy on a mound. It was commissioned by Frederick II when, as Crown Prince, he was garrisoned at Neuruppin in 1732: the temple was the first architectural essay of Georg-Wenzeslas von Knobelsdorff. Immediately below it lies an eccentric formal garden where statues of 16th-century pashas, buccaneers and Indian potentates are supplemented by modern pieces. This formal garden was added in the 19th century by a local shopkeeper Johann-Christian Gentz, who bought the site in 1853 and restored the Musentempel.

The whole of the garden now has a Moorish overlay, which can be seen on the formidable gateway at the southern end, the boundary walls, and several pavilions around the garden, one of which doubles up as a café. This too was the work of the Gentz family, who eventually gave the whole ensemble to the town of Neuruppin as a public park. The formal garden near the entrance has some interesting plantings, including cut-leaved hazels, weeping beech trees, and a few rhododendrons. The garden would benefit from further restoration.

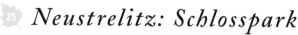

Neustrelitz: Schlosspark

open: All year, daily, dawn to dusk

Location: S of the town centre, well signposted

Further information from:
Schlosspark, 17235-Neustrelitz
Tel: 03981 253119

Nearby sights of interest:
The Orangery on the edge of the park and the nearby Schlosskirche.

The main feature of the Schlosspark at Neustrelitz is a starkly simplified formal garden which runs down from the site of the ducal palace (blown up in 1945) to a Temple of Apollo. The original parterres were altered in the landscape style early in the 19th century: nothing remains except the grass which surrounds their urns and ornaments. These include statues of the angel of "Victory at Leuthen" erected, somewhat belatedly in 1854, to commemorate Frederick the Great's victory over Austria in 1757; and the mythological twins Castor and Pollux. The lime avenue on either side is tapered to create an optical illusion of greater length. The Temple of Apollo is an Ionic temple and it shelters a copy of Canova's statue of Hebe.

To one side of the formal garden is a walk lined with white-painted sandstone statues of gods and seasons. More are housed in the orangery, now a restaurant, which Karl Schinkel redecorated with brilliant colours and furnished with copies of antique and classical statues. Elsewhere in the park is a bust of Blücher, the Prussian marshall, who was a native of Mecklenburg. Beyond it stands a memorial to Queen Luise of Prussia (a Princess of Mecklenburg-Strelitz), in the form of a small Doric temple containing a copy of her original white marble effigy at Charlottenburg. It sits on a mound, flanked by a huge copper beech, in a landscaped English-style park. It is less threadbare than many such landscapes in eastern Germany, although most of the buildings and monuments are, alas, disfigured by graffiti.

Simple elegance now reigns over the grand main axis which was once an elaborate parterre.

Oberhof: Rennsteig Garden

Location: 1km (½ mile) from Oberhof; 31km (19 miles) S of Gotha

open: May to Oct, daily, 9am–6pm (closes 4pm in Oct)

Further information from:
Rennsteiggarten, 98557-Oberhof
Tel: 036842 22245

Nearby sights of interest:
The uplands of Thüringen and the Rennsteig.

This modern alpine botanic garden is unique in Germany. As well as the familiar edelweiss, gentians, pinks, and primulas, the Rennsteig Garden has some 4,000 different alpine plants, including exotica from mountain ranges all over the world. The hub of the garden is a series of landscaped rock gardens. Beds are planted both geographically and geologically: there are areas devoted to chalk-lovers, plants of the alpine meadows, the flora of granite mountains, southern hemisphere alpines, and plants from silicate soils, as well as sections for dwarf rhododendrons, and the medicinal plants of Thüringen.

On the hillside above the main rock gardens, patches of wooded moorland have been cleared and planted with little self-contained gardens, each of which is devoted to the plants of a region, genus or terrain. The Caucasus, the Himalayas, the Rockies, and the Arctic tundra are particularly well represented.

The garden has adapted well to the demands of a consumer-led economy: it is beautifully laid out, well labelled and has instructive boards at crucial vantage points. The seemingly natural setting of all the displays is a particular strength of the garden, while the view of the Thüringer Forest from the top alone is worth the journey. But the most lasting impression is of a beautiful natural hillside where all the alpine flowers of the world have been brought together in one garden of Eden.

A view of the Thüringer Forest from the Rennsteig Garden.

🍁 27 *Potsdam: Babelsberg*

🚃 open: All year, daily, dawn to dusk

🏛 open: Daily: Apr to Oct, 9am–5pm; Nov to Jan, 9am–4pm; Feb and Mar, 9am–3pm

Further information from:
Park Babelsberg
Tel: 0331 291100 (Tourist Office)

Nearby sights of interest:
Schloss Glienicke.

The neo-Norman Schloss at Babelsberg is complemented by a Pleasure Ground in the Victorian style.

Location: First left after Humboldtbrücke into Allee-nach-Glienicke: entrance 2km (1 mile) on the left

This gloriously Gothic garden is as different as can be imagined from the Rococo and neoclassical fancies of Sanssouci (see pp.46–9), and yet Babelsberg is an integral part of the mega-landscape which Peter Joseph Lenné planned for Potsdam and the Havel lakes in the 19th century. When Prince William of Prussia commissioned Karl Schinkel to build the Schloss in 1833, he took such incidents as the Nicolaikirche and his brother Carl's estate at Kleine-Glienicke across the Havel into the borrowed landscape of Babelsberg. Nowadays it enjoys a superb view of the Glienicke Bridge. The imposing Schloss is neo-Norman, built of yellow brick and inspired by Windsor Castle, which King George IV of England had recently restored.

Prince Pückler took charge of the landscaping in 1843 and extended the park until it contained over 200ha (494 acres) in 1867, by which time William was now King William, and shortly to become the first German emperor. It was Prince Pückler who laid out the Pleasure Ground, a gardenesque extravagance of the kind he much favoured. It consists of a sequence of flower beds and panniers, enclosed by palmetto tiles, and richly planted with seasonal bedding, which lines the winding valley down from the schloss. To one side stands the formal rose garden, enclosed within a gilded Gothic metalwork arcade and at the bottom is a circular garden, draped with climbers. Alas, the fountains no longer work as the power house, built as a mock fort down on the lakeside, has not been repaired since 1961.

In the park are many charming buildings. They include the white Kleiner Schlössl, built between 1841 and 1842, the Flatow Tower (1853), and, erected in 1868 to commemorate Bismarck's campaigns, the Siegessäule, whose base is graced by busts of the Chancellor and Prussian generals. Babelsberg is recovering from years of neglect and unchecked growth: clearance and replanting gallop apace.

Potsdam: Neuer Garten

Location: Well signposted in Potsdam

This 122ha (300 acre) park, between the River Havel and the Heiliger See, was purchased by Frederick William II in about 1786. It was first laid out by J A Eyserbeck, but much altered by Peter Joseph Lenné from 1820 onwards. Halfway along the shore of the Heiliger See is the Marmorpalais, begun in 1787, which is visible from such other landmarks as Klein-Glienicke (see p.20). A long avenue of fastigiate oaks leads to it from the gates, past Dutch-style model cottages and through landscaped parkland. Poplars and horse chestnuts run down to the edge of the lake.

The Egyptian-style orangery (1791–92) in front of the Schloss is fronted by a flower garden (1879–80) and boasts an excellent summer display of daturas, oleanders, palms, and pomegranates. The charming formal flower parterre on the garden side of the Marmorpalais has fine summer bedding. Below the Schloss is a kitchen hidden in a ruined temple and connected to the palace by an underground passage. Further follies lie to the north of the Marmorpalais, among them a pyramid which doubles up as an ice-house.

Eventually you come to Cecilienhof, the site of the Potsdam Conference in 1945 but now a smart hotel and restaurant. It was built for Crown Prince William just before the First World War in a school-of-Lutyens neo-Tudor style. Its courtyards are planted with English-style herbaceous borders and yew topiary birds. From here more parkland leads down to the shores of the Havel and the ruins of a shell grotto.

open: All year, daily, dawn to dusk

Further information from:
Neuer Garten, 14469-Potsdam
Tel: 0331 37050 (Schlosshotel Cecilienhof)

Nearby sights of interest:
Sanssouci.

Late-summer bedding in front of the Marmorpalais Orangery.

Potsdam: Sanssouci

open: All year, daily, dawn to dusk. Botanischergarten der Universität Potsdam: daily, 8am–5pm (closes 4pm Oct to Mar)
open: Schloss Sanssouci: Daily: Apr to Sep, 9am–12.30pm and 1–5pm (closes 4pm Feb, Mar and Oct; 3pm Nov to Jan). The Chinesicheshaus: May to Oct, Sat to Thu, 9am–12.30pm and 1.30–5pm

Further information from:
Park Sanssouci, 14469-Potsdam
Tel: Potsdam tourist office
0331 21100

Nearby sights of interest:
The Bildergalerie; the Neue Kammern; the Orangerie; the Neues Palais; the Römische Bäder; Schloss Charlottenhof; the Friedenskirche.

Location: W of the town centre

Sanssouci Park is probably the most rewarding garden in all Germany. It has evolved continuously over the last 250 years, but it was mainly developed by Frederick the Great between 1744 and 1770, Frederick William IV between 1826 and 1860, and finally by Emperor William II between 1902 and 1913. The park of Sanssouci is extensive, nearly 300ha (741 acres), and its main incidents have been exceptionally well joined together by brilliant landscaping. A full day is needed just to see the principal sights of this vast garden.

Start at Schloss Sanssouci. The best approach is along Am Grüben Gitter, between Ebenhech's sphinxes (1755), past the big fountain with its classical statues and excellent seasonal bedding, and up the Weinberg Terraces, whose ranks of vines have long been famous. Each of the six Baroque terraces has

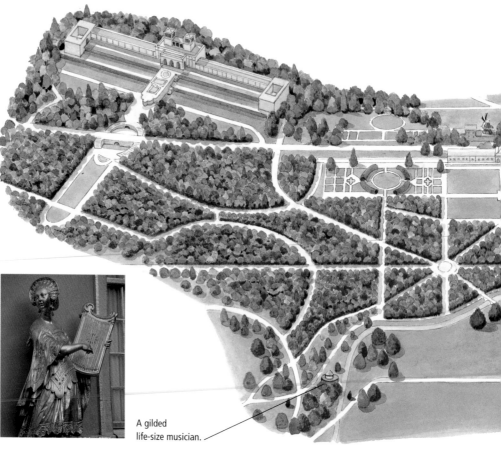

A gilded life-size musician.

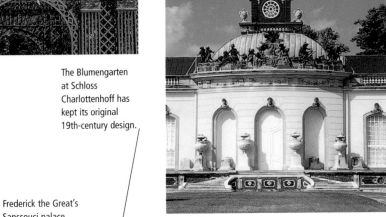

The Blumengarten at Schloss Charlottenhoff has kept its original 19th-century design.

Frederick the Great's Sanssouci palace sits above his vine terraces.

The Bildergallerie looks down over a Dutch garden.

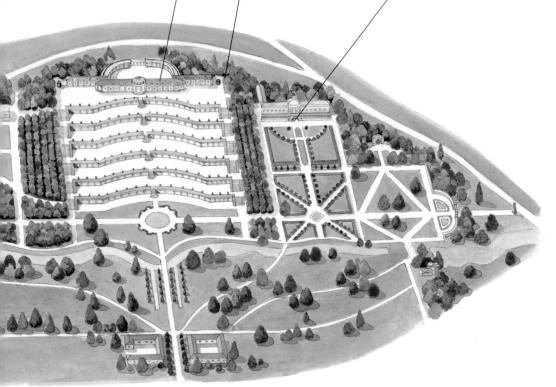

Elegant arbours of gilded metalwork flank the Schloss on Sanssouci's top terrace.

28 glazed doors to trap the sun and help the vines to ripen. Visit the Rococo Schloss, where Frederick the Great lived "without worldly cares" (*sans souci*). To the east is the picture gallery, which overlooks the 18th-century Dutch Garden. Its avenues are lined with lime trees: its hedges are rounded and scalloped. Further to the east is the Neptune Grotto, built between 1751 and 1757, and a flower garden. The obelisk portal at the eastern end has two clusters of pillars guarded by statues of Flora and Pomona. The 2km (1½ mile) Hauptallee runs in a straight line from here to the Baroque Neues Palais – a symbol of Prussian might which commemorates the end of the Seven Years War.

On the hillside to the west of Schloss Sanssouci is the ravishing Sicilian Garden which is formally designed and planted with subtropical exotics. Across the Maulbeerallee lies the Nordic Garden, planted with conifers, ivy, and ferns. Peter Joseph Lenné laid out these two gardens for Frederick William IV in 1857: they are among his last works. Further to the west is the 19th-century orangery, an impressive building inspired by Frederick William's youthful travel in Italy. Allegorical figures fill its niches: look out for Industry, holding a cog-wheel. Tubs with palms, bays, and oranges are positioned along the formal terrace in front. Below the orangery is the stately Jubilee Terrace, built for Emperor William II in 1913. The original parterres have disappeared but a large pool looks down towards a copy of the famous equestrian statue of Frederick the Great. West again of the orangery a long lime avenue leads up towards a ruined Rococo Belvedere (1770). Below it is the Dragon house, of the same period, built in the style of a Chinese pagoda, now used as a café. Frederick William IV laid out the vineyard below the Belvedere. Near the Dragon house is the Spielfestung, a magnificent toy fort built for the sons of William II and fitted with miniature Krupp cannons.

Perhaps the most famous of all the buildings at Sanssouci is the intriguing 18th-century Chinese tea-house, a Rococo fancy with life-size gilded statues of oriental figures and columns which simulate palm trees. To its south is Charlottenhof, built in the 1820s for Frederick William IV as Crown Prince: a pretty neoclassical Karl Schinkel building with a handsome pergola raised up along its southern side. Climbing roses festoon its walls. Behind it lies the Dichterhain, a lawn surrounded by busts of such poets as Goethe, Schiller, and Dante. To the east is a charming flower garden, beautifully planted around a rustic central pergola and full of old rose varieties and colourful bedding.

The Roman Baths on the edge of the nearby lake are built in the style of an Italian villa, and incorporate the Court Gardener's House, a Tea Pavilion, and the Hall of Arcades. All have small but lavish flower gardens, and tender plants are brought here for the summer to intensify the Italian effect. At the south-east of the grounds is the Friedenskirche, a Byzantine church designed for Frederick William IV by Ludwig Persius in the 1840s. The parkland to the west is known as the Marly Garden: it was landscaped by Lenné and elegantly sets off the architecture of the domed church. It was Lenné's genius which welded the whole of Sanssouci together into one fluid design. Sanssouci is widely acclaimed as his masterpiece.

Potsdam's Botanic Garden is a well-maintained enclave within the park. It has collections of Australian plants, conifers and rhododendrons, and a fine ginkgo in the systematic borders. On the other side of the Maulbeerallee are more beds, integrated into the Paradiesgarten, where an enclosed Roman Garden was designed Pompeii-style around a small courtyard. There are some interesting trees here, including x *Sorbopyrus auricularis*, the rare intergeneric cross between a pear and a whitebeam.

Sphinxes flank the main avenue up to Frederick the Great's majestic palace of Sanssouci.

Rheinsberg: Schlosspark

Location: Signposted in the town

open: All year, Tue to Sun, 9.30am–5pm
open: As above

Further information from:
Schloss Rheinsberg,
16831-Rheinsberg
Tel: 033931 2059 (Rheinsberg tourist office)

Nearby sights of interest:
The woods and lakes around Rheinsberg.

Rheinsberg is a large garden of major historical importance which was developed during the period of transition between the Baroque and landscape styles. It is neither extravagant nor dull, just a little eccentric and very harmonious. It was begun in 1736 by Frederick II while Crown Prince of Prussia and became the precursor to Sanssouci (see pp.46–9). To Frederick, and to his friend the architect Knobelsdorf, we owe the island Schloss, the classical Cavalierhaus and the small parterre in front of the Schloss where a statue of Apollo is flanked by the four elements.

The main axis leads out from the Schloss, through an orange parterre where citrus trees are put out for the summer months, up the Sphinx Steps and along to the main entrance gate, which is guarded by statues of the goddesses Flora and Pomona on columns. But most of the garden is the work of Frederick's younger brother Prince Henry, to whom he gave the estate in 1744. Near the orange parterre are a pyramid (Prince Henry's burial place), an outdoor theatre (the Heckentheater, dating from 1758), and a memorial to Prince Henry's and Frederick's younger brother Prince August-Wilhelm (1722–58).

Larch trees frame a view down to Rheinsberg's lake.

Along the all-important main transverse axis, parallel to the lake, is an oval *rond-point* with the Salon, the central building of a former orangery, and statues of the four seasons. Further along, through wood-like groves, is the Egreria Grotto. A second grotto, the Feldsteingrotte, lies on the shore of the lake. English-style landscaping developed around the Baroque outline of the garden.

On the terraced shores of the lake opposite the Schloss is the obelisk which Prince Henry erected in 1791 to commemorate Prince August-Wilhelm and the heroes of the Seven Years War. The whole park is Prince Henry's own monument, witness to the loyalty which characterized his life of service to Prussia.

Sangerhausen: Rosarium

Location: Signposted in the town

This is the greatest rose collection in Germany: of all the rose gardens in the world, only Cavriglia in Italy has more cultivars. It was founded by the German Rose Society in 1898 and opened to the public five years later. As well as providing a test ground for new varieties, it became a repository for almost every new rose introduced into commerce, so that it now boasts more than 6,500 different cultivars and 55,000 rose bushes. It was comparitively well-maintained during the communist years, although unable to acquire all the new varieties introduced between 1950 and 1990. However, as a reference collection of the roses of the first half of the 20th century it is unrivalled – a living encyclopaedia.

Certain classes of roses are particularly well represented, notably polyanthas, hybrid perpetuals, noisette hybrids, and ramblers of every kind. The fluid design carries the visitor around the pool and formal display gardens near the entrance to the garden, where the "black" rose 'Nigrette' and the "green" rose *Rosa chinensis* 'Viridiflora' are displayed as curiosities, up past ranks of ramblers and climbers, through the damasks, bourbons, and *rugosa* hybrids, until rows and rows of early polyantha roses are reached at the top.

Although the Rosarium has some 15ha (37 acres), it feels smaller and more intimate. Space is certainly at a premium, so bush roses are pruned to keep them small and climbers are tied in to a single post. There are some ornamental trees and a small rock garden, but Sangerhausen is above all a wonderful garden in which to study roses and their history. And, of course, to make lists of names that one would like to grow in one's own garden. All the roses are labelled, most of them correctly.

open: Daily: May and Sep, 8am–7pm; Jun to Aug, 8am–8pm

Further information from:
Rosarium Sangerhausen,
Steinberger Weg 3,
06526-Sangerhausen
Tel: 03464 572522

Nearby sights of interest:
Beautiful countryside in the Kyffhäuser Gebirge.

Rosa 'Geschwind's Orden' is one of thousands of climbers in this garden.

Schwerin: Schlossgarten

Location: In the town centre

open: All year, daily, dawn to dusk

open: All year, Tue to Sun, 10am–6pm

Further information from:
Schlossgarten, 19055-Schwerin
Tel: 0385 812314

Nearby sights of interest:
The Gothic Dom, and the Schleifmühle, a half-timbered water mill dating from 1705 in Schwerin.

The ducal schloss at Schwerin fills a small island between the Schweriner See and the Burg See. Its glittering pinnacles recall the French Renaissance châteaux: it would not look out of place in the Loire Valley. There are two historic gardens at Schloss Schwerin: the dramatic 19th-century Burggarten on the Schlossinsel and the bolder, more extensive Baroque garden to which it is linked by a causeway. The Burggarten was made by Peter Joseph Lenné in the 1840s and 1850s. Its spectacular shell fountain, grotto, staircases, arcades, and neoclassical terraces are thought of as his architectural masterpiece. The Baroque garden was laid out on the mainland for Duke Christian Ludwig II of Mecklenburg-Schwerin between 1748 and 1753. The architect was a Frenchman named Jean Legeay who placed a cascade at the furthest end, to create a focal point. The formal gardens near the causeway are now much simplified and reduced, but planted with an edging of seasonal bedding, and dominated by a striking equestrian statue of Duke Friedrich Franz II.

On either side of the formal gardens the ancient tunnels of clipped hornbeam are now very thick, and as much as 6m (20ft) high. The outer edges of the gardens are marked by avenues of lime trees and long canals. Most of the space between the causeway and the cascade is filled with a formal water parterre lined with sandstone statues. They are all copies of the originals placed here in 1752. A garden pavilion was made to one side of the long axis in 1818. The space behind it was then laid out in the 1840s as a landscape garden. But this area is only of secondary importance to the Burggarten and Baroque garden, which is the most extensive in Mecklenburg-Pommern.

The glittering pinnacles of Schloss Schwerin are matched by the extravagant water parterre.

Weimar: Belvedere

Location: Well signposted from the town centre

The Baroque Schloss Belvedere sits on a ridge, from where there are stunning views north towards Weimar. It was built between 1724 and 1732 by J A Richter, who also laid out the garden in the formal style. The conservatory dates from the 1740s and by 1820 the garden as a whole housed nearly 8,000 taxa: Goethe was personally involved in enlarging the plant collections. In 1766 Duchess Anna Amelia demolished the wall between the parterres and the woodlands to the south of the Schloss. She planted a Giant Avenue through the woods and made a lake at the bottom: it was plied by gondolas, housed in the grotto. Duke Karl August redesigned the park in the landscape style from 1780 onwards. It now totals some 41ha (101 acres) and its condition is at last improving after years of neglect. Within it are fine specimen trees and beautiful meadows, which create a sense of great peace.

The pretty circular Rose Garden was remade in 1994 according to a design by the English landscaper Humphry Repton, with honeysuckle growing on the pillars and box-edged beds of modern roses in the middle: historically incorrect, but agreeable. Additions made in the 19th century include the Russian Garden (1810), the small garden theatre (1823) and a small maze (1843). On the western side of the maze is a tunnel of pleached hornbeams, which makes a delightful cool alley in summer.

The whole park was rearranged between 1843 and 1850 in its present form when the large flower garden to the south of the conservatory was laid out. Exotic plants – notably big palms and yuccas – are still put out here for the summer and supplemented by lavish plantings of summer bedding. Belvedere is the busiest of the Weimar gardens.

open: All year, daily, dawn to dusk

open: Apr to Oct, Tue to Sun, 10am–6pm

Further information from:
Schloss Belvedere, Weimar

Nearby sights of interest:
Weimar.

One of several reconstructed formal gardens near the Schloss at Belvedere.

open: All year, daily, dawn to dusk

Further information from:
Park an der Ilm, Weimar

Nearby sights of interest:
The Goethehaus: All year, daily, 9am to 12 noon and 1–5pm (closes 4pm in winter).

Weimar: Park an der Ilm

Location: On the edge of the town: well-signposted

The Park an der Ilm was Goethe's major essay in landscaping, though he was encouraged and assisted throughout by his friend and patron Duke Karl August of Saxe-Weimar. Indeed, the Duke was the principal mover behind the creation of an integrated design for the park, which actually extends to no more than 50ha (124 acres), but seems much larger because of its position on either side of a long valley.

Goethe laid out the park in the German landscape style between 1777 and 1778. He also designed the Roman House in 1792 as a summer residence for the Duke. It recalls the Roman villas that Goethe saw during his travels in Italy and, being built high above the valley, dominates much of the park. But it is the Arcadian landscape of the park itself that is the great attraction of this classically peaceful and beautiful valley. It was later worked on by Eduard Petzold (c1850) though much of the damage done in 1945 has yet to be repaired. On one edge of the valley is Goethe's Gartenhaus where he lived during the first six years of his stay at Weimar and which later served as his summer residence. The garden has been charmingly restored with simple plantings of the roses and herbaceous plants which Goethe grew or referred to in his writings and studies. The Goethe gardens here and in Weimar itself are best seen in early summer when the old-fashioned roses are in bloom.

Old roses from Goethe's day adorn his cottage garden in Park an der Ilm.

Weimar: Tiefurt

Location: About 6km (4 miles) E of the town

open: All year, daily, dawn to dusk

open: All year, Tue to Sun, 9am–1pm, 2–5pm (Nov to Feb until 4pm)

Further information from:
Schloss Tiefurt, Weimar

Nearby sights of interest:
Weimar.

The park at Schloss Tiefurt was laid out for the Duchess Anna Amelia, who used the modest Schloss as her summer residence between 1781 and 1806. Anna Amelia was a Princess from Brunswick and a niece of Frederick II of Prussia. Widowed at 19, she acted as regent for her son Karl August during his long minority. She wrote of Tiefurt: "I want to put the gardens in such a state as Fauns and Nymphs would not be ashamed to inhabit." The result is 16ha (40 acres) of spacious, classical German landscape, occupying a huge semicircular curving valley, its meadows, the River Ilm and the slopes beyond.

Clumps of trees are used to set off the space, create surprises and provide a setting for the monuments. The latter are quite modest: among the most interesting are the Monument to Mozart and the Muses (1799), the Temple of the Muses (1803), the Muse of the Sublime, and the early 19th-century classical tea-house. The park was partially reworked in the late landscape style by Eduard Petzold during the 1840s with help from Prince Pückler, but the whole park is now in need of restoration.

Stately landscape plantings in the valley at Tiefurt.

Key to gardens

1. Ansbach: **Hofgarten**
2. Augsburg: **Botanic Garten**
3. Baden-Baden: **Kurpark and Lichtentalerallee**
4. Bamberg: **Seehof**
5. Bayreuth: **Eremitage**
6. Bruchsal: **Schlossgarten**
7. Chiemsee: **Schloss Herrenschiemsee**
8. Coburg: **Schloss Rosenau**
9. Erlangen: **Botanic Garten**
10. Ettal: **Schloss Linderhof**
11. Frieburg: **Botanic Garten**
12. Freising: **Sichtungsgarten Weihenstephan**
13. Heidelberg: **Botanic Garten and Schlosspark**
14. Karlsruhe: **Schlossgarten and Botanic Garten**
15. Karlsruhe: **Stadtgarten**
16. Lahr: **Stadtpark**
17. Ludwigsburg: **Schlossgarten**
18. Mainau: **Insel Mainau**
19. Munich: **Botanic Garten**
20. Munich: **Englischergarten**
21. Munich: **Nymphenburg**
22. Munich: **Schloss Schleissheim and Schloss Lustheim**
23. Munich: **Westpark**
24. Nürnberg: **Patrizierschloss Neunhof**
25. Pforzheim: **Alpengarten**
26. Rastatt: **Schloss Favorite**
27. Rastatt: **Schlossgarten and Pagodenburg**
28. **Sanspareil**
29. Schönbusch: **Park**
30. Schwetzingen: **Schlossgarten**
31. Stuttgart: **Hohenheim**
32. Stuttgart: **Killesberg Park**
33. Stuttgart: **Park Wilhelma**
34. Tübingen: **Botanic Garten**
35. Veitshöchheim: **Hofgarten**
36. Weikersheim: **Schlossgarten**
37. Weinheim: **Hermannshoft**
38. Weinheim: **Schlosspark and Exotenwald**
39. Würzburg: **Botanic Garten**
40. Würzburg: **Hofgarten**
41. Würzburg: **Okogarten**

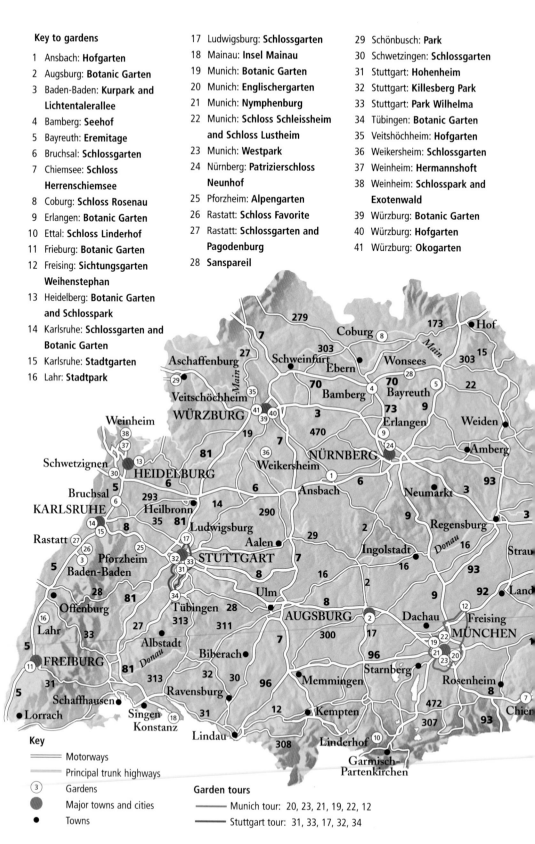

Key

═══ Motorways
═══ Principal trunk highways
③ Gardens
⬤ Major towns and cities
● Towns

Garden tours

── Munich tour: 20, 23, 21, 19, 22, 12
── Stuttgart tour: 31, 33, 17, 32, 34

Southern Germany

The gardens of southern Germany tend to be clustered around the old princely courts. This is especially true of Munich and Stuttgart, but also of Bayreuth and those parts of the old Palatinate which are now in Baden. All these gardens are dominated by the grand layouts of the great dynastic families. The sheer size of Schleissheim (see p.79) and Nymphenburg (see p.78) tells you all you need to know about the self-importance of the various branches of the Wittelsbach family. Ludwigsburg (see p.71) near Stuttgart is no less impressive.

The Baroque tradition is well represented in southern Germany. Every ruler was dazzled by Versailles and wanted to outshine King Louis XIV. Nymphenburg in Munich is among the better known examples but "Mad" King Ludwig II of Bavaria was actually building an exact replica of the gardens and palace of Versailles at Schloss Herrenchiemsee (see p.64) as late as 1880.

Other rulers, notably the imperial Prince Bishops, were exponents of the Baroque variant that is known as Rococo, and they bequeathed some of its best monuments to us: there is nothing to match the wit and

The Temple of Friendship lies deep in the woods at Schönbusch.

Deggendorf

Passau

5

20

A Gouberaut statue of Mercury stands above the great Baroque garden of Seehof.

invention of Seehof or the Hofgarten in Veitshöchheim (see pp.62 and 94) in all France or Italy, let alone in northern Germany. It is in the south that we see the Rococo at its most developed and beguiling. Gardens here are more exuberant than in the rest of Germany and are built to amuse, as well as to impress. There is none of the cold classicism of Prussia in the gardens of Baden and Bavaria.

Gardeners and landscapers in both the 18th and 19th centuries attracted a considerable following. When the Elector Karl Theodor of the Palatinate succeeded to the throne of Bavaria in 1777, he took his designer and landscaper Friedrich Ludwig von Sckell with him from Schwetzingen to Munich. Despite Sckell's important contribution to the layout of the Englischer Garten in Munich (see p.77), the south of Germany is not the best place to study the landscape movement. The only exceptions to this rule are provided by the gardens of pocket-sized principalities, such as Bayreuth, often ruled by Protestant families. In fact, the landscape style exists principally in those parts of the country which joined Bavaria comparatively recently, such as Schönbusch near Aschaffenburg (see p.85), and Sanspareil near Bayreuth (see p.84). There are fewer botanic gardens in the south than in the rest of Germany, though the magnificent one at Munich owes its size and competence to the need to develop a showpiece for the important kingdom of Bavaria. Augsburg Botanic Garden (see p.60) is as

The pool at the heart of Heidelberg's new Botanic Garden.

much a show garden and teaching garden as a botanical institute: its combination of scholarship with civic amenity is unusual in southern Germany.

The two greatest experimental horticultural stations in the whole of Germany are in the south: Sichtungsgarten Weihenstephan in Bavaria (see p.67) and Hermannshof in Baden (see p.96).

The Temple of Apollo at
Schwetzingen, topped
by a golden sun.

There are good examples of the new German style of
planting at Westpark in Munich (see p.80), Killesberg
Park in Stuttgart (see p.91) and the Okogarten at
Würzburg (see p.99). Some of the historic gardens have
been turned into tourist attractions, but most have been
passed to the state and are maintained by foundations set
up to manage the cultural patrimony of the country.

Southern Germany is made for tourism. The gentle
rolling countryside is most attractive, while the pine-
covered hills of the Black Forest and the German Alps
have long been famous. The settings for such gardens as
Schloss Linderhof in the Alps (see p.66) and Mainau on
Lake Constance (see pp.72–5) are exquisite. Summer
temperatures are among the warmest in central Europe.
Roads in the south are good, though traffic jams on the
motorways can play havoc with your timings. There are
wonderful historic towns to visit – Bamberg, Heidelberg
and Freising to name a few – and you can be certain
of whole-hearted hospitality in every part of the region.

Ansbach: Hofgarten

Location: In the town centre

open: All year, daily, dawn to dusk

Further information from:
Hofgarten, 91522-Ansbach

Nearby sights of interest:
The Residenz is worth visiting, especially the Fayencenzimmer and the Spiegelkabinett.

The 17ha (42 acre) Hofgarten is a good example of a well-kept municipal park. It was substantially laid out in the first half of the 18th century and remade after 1945 in its present, rather simplified, form. The pretty, old orangery was made by Karl Friedrich von Zocha. The formal garden in front of it has neatly planted bright bedding and pots with orange trees are positioned here for the summer. Nearby are two squares of closely-cropped lime trees, known as the Lindensalen: each has a fountain in the middle and makes a shady place to walk in summer. The rose garden has box-edged compartments around a circular fountain and modern roses: tubs of agapanthus and agaves are put out for the summer. All around is the park laid out with leafy avenues of lime, one of which is over 250 years old.

Augsburg: Botanic Garden

Location: Next to the zoo, follow the signs

open: Daily: 1 May to 15 Aug, 9am–9pm; Apr and 16 Aug to 30 Sep, 9am–8pm; Mar and 16 to 30 Sep, 9am–6pm; 1 Oct to 28 Feb, 9am–5pm

Further information from:
Botanischer Lehr- und Schaugarten, Dr. Ziegenspeck Weg 10, 86161 Augsburg
Tel: 0821 3246038

Nearby sights of interest:
The old centre of Augsburg.

Augsburg's Botanic Garden calls itself a botanic, teaching and show garden: it is an excellent example of a modern German garden which seeks to combine scholarship with civic amenity. Founded in 1933 to replace the older Botanic Garden in the city centre, the garden was completely redesigned and replanted in the 1980s. Only a few trees, including a specimen of *Phellodendron amurense* remain from the pre-war plantings. Today the garden consists of many well-maintained habitats and incidents, which lead naturally into each other. A great number of ideas have been developed within the garden and make it highly instructive.

The entrance avenue passes between pollarded robinias underplanted with seasonal bedding. To one side is a series of designer layouts suitable for small modern gardens: these are typical of the botanic garden as a whole, which is intended to show local people what they can do to plan and plant their own gardens. A model kitchen garden is laid out in a rondel shape with a small pool in the middle. Beyond is a sunken area where spring bulbs, annuals, and bedding plants are displayed in plots according to the season. Nearby is a Japanese garden with clipped shrubs, landscaped streams and waterfalls. Further on are a modern rose garden, a steppe garden, a rock garden, a fern garden, a medicinal herb garden and a water garden. The glasshouses include a "Victoriahaus", where *Victoria amazonica* is grown every year from seed, and a tall tropical palm house.

Fine bedding and herbaceous plantings at Augsburg's well-maintained Botanic Garden.

Baden-Baden: Kurpark and Lichtentalerallee

Location: In the town centre

Baden-Baden developed as a fashionable spa in the 19th century: the Kurhaus dates from 1821 and the Trinkhalle, from where the waters were drunk, from 1839. That was also the year when the beautiful public gardens were first laid out along the river banks. Much of the Lichtentalerallee was landscaped between 1850 and 1870, while the Gönneranlage (see below) was laid out by Max Läuger in 1909.

So much for the history: Baden-Baden offers some of the most stunning and extensive parks and gardens in Germany. Above all, it is the stately disposition of beautiful trees along the valley bottom which gives them their form and quality. Among the most handsome specimens are gingkos, gleditsias, fastigiate oaks, *Populus lasiocarpa*, sequoias, tulips trees and many different cultivars of beech, while the rarities include *Acer platanoides* 'Reitenbachii' and *Aesculus hippocastanum* 'Umbraculifera'. Mounds of rhododendrons grow on shady banks and slopes.

The Gönneranlage is a series of formal gardens, most of them with mature roses. As well as beds of hybrid teas and floribundas, there are climbing roses on pergolas and a magnificent pair of standard *Rosa* 'Leverkusen' flanking the central garden.

open: All year, daily, dawn to dusk

Further information from:
Kurpark and Lichtentalerallee,
76530-Baden-Baden
Tel: 07221 275200 (Baden-Baden tourist office)

Nearby sights of interest:
The Kurhaus and casino; pure gold roulette table in the Wintergarten.

Fountains and sculptures in Gönneranlage's rose garden.

Bamberg: Seehof

Location: 3km (2 miles) E of Bamberg

open: May to Nov, Mon to Fri, 7am–6pm (closes 6pm Oct and 5pm Nov to Mar); Sat, Sun and Public Holidays, 10.30am–7pm; Nov to Apr closes Sat, Sun and Public Holidays
open: As above

Further information from:
Schlosspark Seehof,
96117-Memmelsdorf

Nearby sights of interest:
The buildings of Bamberg.

The great castle-palace of Seehof was built by Marquard von Stauffenberg, Prince-Bishop of Bamberg, between 1683 and 1693, but it was his successors who lavished such attention on the gardens that they came to rival Veitshöchheim (see p.94). Nor does the similarity end there: the owners of Seehof employed the same master-sculptor Ferdinand Dietz to furnish amusing statues for both palaces. Seehof once boasted some 400 of them, though almost all are lost. The gardens reached their peak under Prince-Bishop Adam Friedrich von Seinsheim (1757–79). By then they were 600m (1,969ft) long and 350m (1,148ft) wide, laid out as a huge series of formal gardens on an irregular grid. They represented the highest state of sophistication ever reached by the Rococo, long after most of Germany had been swept up by the landscape movement.

The gardens began to disintegrate with the Napoleonic wars, but were never converted to an English landscape style. Little but the structural outline now remains, and that only because of the restoration undertaken since the Bavarian state acquired it in 1976. The main avenues and hedges are again in place and the centrepiece of the great cascade has been restored. Some of the statues have been recovered or copied, and painted in their original white and gold. And the work continues.

The great cascade in front of the palace has recently been restored.

Bayreuth: Eremitage

Location: 4km (2½ miles) E of the city, rather badly signposted

Three periods of garden history are represented in the Eremitage's 50ha (124 acres). The first is the age of the formal gardens: the extensive geometrical hedges and water gardens were originally laid out between 1718 and 1726 for Margrave Georg Wilhelm of Bayreuth. Some of the formal compartments are planted with flower gardens and fruit trees: a hornbeam tunnel runs along their north-eastern side. It was Georg Wilhelm too who first worked on the old Schloss. In front of it lies a flowery parterre and, beyond, a long steep watercourse which crashes down the hillside to the River Main below.

The second and most significant period in the history of the Eremitage is the 1740s, when both the Schloss and the gardens were developed by Princess Wilhelmina. During this time a series of follies was built below the old Schloss. The only two to survive are the Untere Grotte and a theatre built as a Roman ruin. Then, in 1749, a new Schloss was built next to the old one. Its focal point is a free-standing octagonal temple of the sun, glittering with glass and gold. Its dome is crowned by a gilded statue of Apollo and his horse-drawn chariot. On either side of the temple are colonnaded curving wings, which enclose a pool with spectacular fountains and statues known as the Obere Grotte. The third period in the Eremitage's history is the 19th-century English-style landscaping, with cool woodlands, fine trees, lush meadows and purple rhododendrons.

open: All year, daily, dawn to dusk
open: Apr to Sep, Tue to Sun, 9–11.30am and 1pm–4.30pm; Oct to Mar, Tue to Sun, 10–11.30am and 1–2.30pm. Guided tours only

Further information from:
Eremitage, 95444-Bayreuth
Tel: Bayreuth tourist office
0921 88560

Nearby sights of interest:
The Altstadt; the Hofgarten.

The front of the new Schloss overlooks Obere Grotte.

Bruchsal: Schlossgarten

Location: In the town centre

The palace at Bruchsal is one of the most important buildings in the history of the Baroque. Its central staircase, by Balthasar Neumann, is a masterpiece. The garden is no more than an adjunct to the palace, but merits a quick visit: both have been well restored since the last war.

In front of the palace are two quincunxes with fountains in the middle, edged in box. The pool and fountains on the terrace behind the house lead down to the white balustrade: two former orangeries flank its edges. A venerable catalpa near the palace leans at an angle of 30°. The main avenue leads away from the garden to the west, lined by statues and double avenues of horse chestnuts. The view back to the palace, particularly when the fountains are playing, is nothing less than enchanting.

open: All year, daily, dawn to dusk
open: All year, Tue to Sun, 9am–1pm and 2–5pm

Further information from:
Schlossgarten, 76646-Bruchsal
Tel: 07251 72771

Nearby sights of interest:
Visit the Schloss itself, a masterpiece of Baroque.

open: Daily: Apr to Sep, 9am–5pm; Oct to Mar, 10am–4pm
open: As above

Further information from:
Schloss Herrenchiemsee,
83256-Chiemsee
Tel: Prien tourist office
08051 83209

Nearby sights of interest:
The Schloss; the island's simple old cathedral.

The Herrenchiemsee statues are copies of originals at Versailles.

Chiemsee: Schloss Herrenchiemsee

Location: Ferry from Prien

Schloss Herrenchiemsee was Ludwig II's new Versailles: it was the most expensive, if not the most extravagant, of his fantasy building projects. Not only did Ludwig copy the palace exactly, but he also set out to remake Louis XIV's gardens and park.

The fountains are the chief glory of Herrenchiemsee, and flow for short periods twice an hour all through the day. The centrepiece is the Latona Fountain, a tiered confection of spouts, ringed with small lead statues of frogs and tortoises. Around it are modern baroque parterres richly planted in summer with begonias, cannas, standard fuchsias and lantanas. On the upper terrace, by the Schloss, two even larger tanks each have a rocky pyramid as their main feature: one is topped by Fortune and the other by Fame, who is riding a horse and blowing her trumpet from which a huge plume of water spouts high into the sky.

The park occupies the whole island and the palace its highest point. Long, broad drives run down a double avenue to the lake on the eastern side and across the terraces, down a lime avenue and over a short canal to the lake on the western side. There is a 2km (1½ mile) walk from the landing stage to the Schloss and back, though horse-drawn drays will take you there at a price.

open: All year, daily, dawn to dusk
open: All year, Tue to Sun, 10–11.30am and 1.30–4.30pm (closes 3.45pm in winter). Guided tours only

Further information from:
Schloss Rosenau, 96472-Rödental

Nearby sights of interest:
The Museum of Glass.

Coburg: Schloss Rosenau

Location: 7km (4¼ miles) NE of Coburg

Schloss Rosenau was built for Duke Ernst I of Saxe-Coburg between 1808 and 1817 according to plans by Karl Schinkel. Prince Albert the "uncrowned king of England" was born here in 1819. The charm of Rosenau lies in its open grassy spaces and deciduous woodland. Below the Schloss is a long open meadow, rich in wild plants and particularly lovely in mid-spring when the buttercups flower, and in early summer when the meadow is blue with *Geranium pratense*. Large clumps of woodland frame the sides of the meadow. The grounds include a lake, a grotto, a sundial and an old orangery, now a museum of modern glass. A visit to Rosenau is essential for anyone who wishes to understand the liberal education enjoyed by the prince who played such an important part in the history of the British monarchy. Queen Victoria herself said of Rosenau: "Were I not who I am, I would live here forever". Many visitors would still say the same today.

Erlangen: Botanic Garden

Location: In the town centre

Originally founded in 1626 as a *Hortus Medicus* the botanic garden moved to its present site at the edge of the old Schlossgarten in 1828. It is one of the smallest botanic gardens in Germany and therefore one of the easiest to enjoy. Since its 2ha (5 acres) support some 4,000 taxa, it is also a model for fitting as much as possible into a small space. The garden has two distinctive features. The first is its neatness and exceptionally high standard of maintenance, and the second is its submission to horticultural aesthetics: whatever the scientific lesson to impart, there are attractive arrangements of plants.

The collections are numerous: among them are a Steppe garden, systematic beds for water plants, moorland vegetation, bog plants, coastal plants, a fern garden, an extensive physic garden, natural shrubby Mediterranean vegetation, a model kitchen garden and a herb garden. Small woodland areas are planted with natural mixtures of trees, including oak and birch, oak and hornbeam, and native conifers. The rock garden is planted mainly geographically but also geologically. Another particularly interesting garden is devoted to subalpine plants, such as alchemillas and astrantias. The glasshouses include a good modern collection of Canary Islands plants, an alpine house, and houses for tropical and subtropical water plants such as *Nelumbo nucifera*. The university publishes a comprehensive series of guides to the garden and its collections. The adjoining Schlossgarten is a pleasant public park with cheerful bedding around the grand fountain in front of the Schloss.

open: All year, daily, 8am–4pm; (closes at 12 noon Sun and Public Holidays in winter). Glasshouses open: Daily except Mon, 9.30–11.30am and 1.30–3pm; (open mornings only in winter)

Further information from:
Botanischer Garten der Universität Erlangen-Nürnberg, Loschgestr. 3, 91054-Erlangen
Tel: 09131 852669

Nearby sights of interest:
The university town of Erlangen.

Neatness and economy of space in Erlangen's systematic beds for water plants.

open: All year, daily, dawn to dusk

open: Apr to Sep, daily, 9am–12.15pm and 12.45–5.30pm; Oct to Mar, daily, 10am–12.15pm and 12.45–4pm

Further information from:
Schloss Linderhof, 82488-Ettal
Tel: 08822 3534 (Ettal tourist office)

Nearby sights of interest:
King Ludwig II's castle at Hohenschwangau.

Ludwig II's Turkish Mosque on the mountain behind Linderhof.

Ettal: Schloss Linderhof

Location: 11km (7 miles) W of Ettal

Theatrical is the word for Ludwig II's Linderhof: the whole ensemble owes more to stage design than to architecture. The Schloss is a tiny, Rococo, frothy extravaganza in brilliant white. It is escapist and in no sense grand. The grounds were laid out by Carl von Effner, the Bavarian royal court gardener, and begun in 1870. The pool in front of the palace has a gilded sculpture of the goddess Flora and *putti* from which a fountain rises almost 30m (98ft). Beyond lie the terraced gardens which ascend steeply to the Temple of Venus at the top, past ornamental flower beds, pots filled with summer bedding and a large bust of Queen Marie Antoinette. Behind the palace a long cascade runs down from an orangery high up the mountain. The statue of Neptune at the bottom is based on the original at Versailles.

To the sides of the Schloss are further formal gardens, exquisitely proportioned and bordered by trellis work. One has gilded statues of Fame and Cupid, and a large terracotta bust of Louis XIV, as well as majolica vases topped by *putti*. The other has a gilded statue of Cupid in the centre of its pool, and leads on out to the park where flowery alpine meadows have been modelled in the English style. At one corner of the park sits a small white mosque with gilded domes, incongruously set against the backdrop of snowy Alps. It was originally designed for the International Exhibition in Paris in 1867: Ludwig II added a recess to hold his peacock throne. Linderhof is by far the most charming of the king's many palaces and gardens.

Freiburg: Botanic Garden

Location: Close to the city centre

open: All year, daily, 10am–6pm

Further information from:
Botanischer Garten der Universität, Schänzelstr. 1, 79104-Freiburg im Breisgau
Tel: 0761 2032877

Nearby sights of interest:
The Minster church.

The botanic garden was founded in 1620 but relocated to its present 2ha (5 acre) site in 1912. Although it has many of the traditional features of botanic gardens it specializes in plantings that illustrate the evolution of the plant kingdom. A collection of ferns is at one end of the trail, and a selection of vine cultivars is at the other. In between are some 8,000 taxa, including fine old conifers and handsome established plants of *Prunus lusitanica* and *Fagus sylvatica* f. *fastigiata*.

The traditional 'Alpinum' has been laid out geographically and ecologically, according to the habitats of alpine plants. The garden has a particularly good collection of plants from eastern Asia and North America, including *Sassafras albidus* and several species of *Carya*. The range of glasshouses includes a tropical house, a subtropical water lily house, a succulent house and a fern house. Here too the theme is evolution: primitive plants like cycads illustrate the early stages, while recent developments are represented by such economic plants as cotton. The succulent house serves to display the principles of biological convergence, whereby the different kinds of cacti and succulents, botanically quite distinct and unrelated, show the same adaptations to changes in climate even though they come from such different parts of the world as central America and southern Africa.

Freising: Sichtungsgarten Weihenstephan

Location: Signposted from Freising

open: Apr to Oct, daily, 8am–6pm (opens 9am Sat and Sun)

Further information from:
Sichtungsgarten
Tel: 08161 713371

Nearby sights of interest:
Freising (the Dom) and Weihenstefan (the Brauerei).

This great experimental and teaching garden attached to Munich university is the leading station in the country for horticultural trials of every kind. Thousands of varieties of plants are grown and tested in the garden for their suitability in cultivation, their compatibility in growing conditions, and their contrasts and harmonies of form and colour.

Students are encouraged to identify not only the names and features of plants, but also the manner in which they can be combined to good effect in private gardens and public parks. Groupings of plants are grown in long experimental beds. The combinations may consist of two complementary plants, for example orange nasturtiums with purple buddleias, or a more complex alliance of many harmonious shapes and shades, such as orange lilies, yellow kniphofias, yellow eremurus and *Euphorbia griffithii* 'Fireglow' set against grey-blue catmint and grasses. In addition to extensive collections of hemerocallis and paeonies, the garden has large areas of shrubs, heathers, ornamental trees, potentillas, as well as a rock garden and steppe-heathland, collections of shade-loving plants and roses.

Experimental flower combinations on a magnificent scale are tried out at Weihenstephan

Visitors should see the Oberdieck Garden, whose layout includes an apothecary's garden, a rhododendron garden and a scented garden, the Model Allotment Gardens and the Show Garden. Weihenstefan repays detailed study by visitors who are themselves keen gardeners.

open: All year, daily, dawn to dusk

Further information from:
Botanischer Garten der Universität, Im Neuenheimer Feld 340, 69120-Heidelberg
Tel: 06221 565783

Nearby sights of interest:
The city centre of Heidelberg, especially the old university quarter.

Heidelberg Castle seen from near the Schlosspark.

Heidelberg: Botanic Garden and Schlosspark

Location: In the new university campus

The main reason for visiting the Schlosspark, apart from some tall cedars and wellingtonias, is to enjoy the dizzy vantage-point at the far end of the garden. The view of Heidelberg encompasses the city, the River Neckar, its bridges, the huge red sandstone castle and the wooded hills beyond. Little has survived of the *Hortus Palatinus*, the gardens and waterworks described by 17th-century writers as the "eighth wonder of the world", which Salomon de Caus began to lay out for Frederick V of the Palatinate in 1615. All that remains is the statue of Father Rhine, old and feeble, recumbent on a rocky bed in the midst of a pool where fountain jets spew over him. And even this is a modern copy in epoxy resin.

Heidelberg Botanic Garden has been on its present 4ha (10 acre) site at the heart of the new university campus since 1960. In addition to systematic beds, it offers collections of herbs, medicinal plants, moorland plants, the heathland flora of Lower Saxony, north German coastal plants, and the sand-dune flora of nearby Sandhausen. There are extensive greenhouses for ferns, tropical orchids, Mediterranean plants, bromeliads, palms, bamboos and tropical fruits, and two succulent houses, one for New World and the other for South African cacti and succulents. The "Victoriahaus" contains *Nelumbo nucifera*, *Victoria cruciana* and a collection of tropical insectivorous *Aristolochia* species.

Karlsruhe: Schlossgarten and Botanic Garden

Location: In the city centre

The Schlossgarten was laid out by the Elector Carl Wilhelm von Baden-Durlach in 1715. The original circular design had 32 avenues radiating out from the central tower. However, the purity of this design has been lost through the years. It was last altered for the Bundesgartenschau in 1967 when some attempt was made to integrate modern design and materials within a historic garden. Some of the surviving features are still striking, including the green theatre whose hornbeam hedges are cut at a height which steadily reduces from 6 to 2.5m (19½ to 8ft). It also boasts some good ornamental trees.

The well-maintained 2ha (5 acre) botanic garden adjoins the Schlossgarten. There is a pretty collection of acacias, cordylines, oleanders, *Osmanthus burkwoodii*, palms and *Pittosporum tobira*, which are put out in huge tubs and casks for the summer, while the mild climate of Karlsruhe enables *Poncirus trifoliata* to grow outside all year. The long lean-to Grosses Glashaus consists of three sections. The cactus house has magnificent specimens of *Cereus peruviana* 'Monstrosus', *Echinocactus grusonii* and *Euphorbia grandicornis*, as well as a small collection of carnivorous plants. In the tropical house are begonias, caladiums, heliconias and orchids. Another glasshouse, damaged in the war was converted to a restaurant and café, while the old orangery now houses the state's fine art collection.

open: All year, daily, dawn to dusk. Glasshouses open: All year, daily (except Sat and Public Holidays), 8am–6pm (closes 3.30pm or 4.30pm Sun)

open: All year, Tue to Sun, 10am–5pm (closes 8pm Wed)

Further information from:
Schlossgarten and Botanischer Garten, Hans-Thoma-Strasse 6, 76131-Karlsruhe
Tel: 0721 6082145

Nearby sights of interest:
The Landesmuseum in the Schloss; the Kunsthalle.

Neat, ornamental plantings front the glasshouses in Karlsruhe's Botanic Garden.

open: May to Sep, daily,
8am–6.30pm; Nov to Apr 9am
to sunset

Further information from:
Stadtgarten, 76137-Karlsruhe
Tel: 0721 1336801

Nearby sights of interest:
The sights of Karlsruhe by the
schloss; the Museum Am
Friedrichsplatz.

 # 15 *Karlsruhe: Stadtgarten*

Location: Opposite the main railway station

The Stadtgarten is long and narrow, and appears to lie within a
gentle landscaped hollow. It was considerably changed for the
Bundesgartenschau in 1967, when the two lakes were joined by
a canal. Although principally a colourful public park, extremely
popular at weekends for its children's playgrounds, chessboard,
open air theatre and boat-rides, it also has gardens of horticultural
interest. The attractions include excellent rhododendrons,
magnificent bedding, a modern rose garden, a paeony garden,
and a long arcade with clematis, laburnum, lonicera, wisteria
and other climbing plants. The Japanese garden has stones and
shingle on the lake shore, separated from a more substantial
Japanese garden across the main pathway: here are cherries,
azaleas, stone lanterns and red lacquer gateways. It was the first
Japanese garden to be built in Germany after the war.

open: All year, daily,
8am–7pm (or dusk, if earlier);
(closes 9pm Jul and Aug)

Further information from:
Stadtpark, 77933-Lahr
Tel: 07821 282286

Nearby sights of interest:
The Münster church at Ettenheim,
18km (11 miles) SW of the town.

Traditional patterns of bedding
plants pay tribute to the bust
of Prince Bismarck.

16 *Lahr: Stadtpark*

Location: 1km (½ mile) from the town centre

This is a fine example of the municipal parks which are such a
splendid feature of the German horticultural tradition. The
house and garden – neither of them large or grand – were
bequeathed to the town of Lahr by Christian Wilhelm Jamm in
1875. Within the structure of a 19th-century park, the authorities
create seasonal effects with colourful bedding plants, particularly
near the house and around a bust of Bismarck. Daffodils, tulips
and pansies in spring are followed by begonias, geraniums and
African marigolds in summer and autumn, when the displays are
augmented by a large number of tender plants put outside for
the season. These include palms, huge tree-like oleanders,
banana trees, standard lantanas, and an entire
garden planted with cacti and succulents.

In the rose garden are some 250 cultivars,
mostly modern. It is designed Bagatelle-style
with cones of neatly clipped yew and small beds
rising from grass parterres. Inside the nearby
conservatory is a small collection of cactus and
houseplants. The park has some fine trees,
including planes, limes (don't miss the vast *Tilia
tomentosa*), a magnificent weeping beech and
other beech cultivars. The rhododendrons and
azaleas make an attractive display in late spring.

Ludwigsburg: Schlossgarten

Location: In the town centre

The gardens at Ludwigsburg date from the reign of Duke Eberhard Ludwig (1704–1733). It was he who built the enormous palace and first laid out the extensive grounds. They have, however, been so altered over the years that it is best to describe the numerous attractions of Schlossgarten Ludwigsburg as a historic park with a public spectacle grafted on.

Schlossgarten Ludwigsburg is best entered from the south, where there is a spectacular view over the vast southern parterre. Its sides are edged with chestnut avenues, while brightly coloured roses fill many of the parterres and beds. Others are planted with multi-coloured bedding. Two smaller gardens flank the extensive wings of the palace: the Friedrichsgarten (once the private garden of the dukes and king) and the Mathildengarten (laid out as an English flower garden in the 19th century).

Down to one side is the Upper East Garden, approached by an avenue of plane trees underscored with massed plantings of deep mauve busy lizzies. At the end lie extensive herbaceous plantings in the modern style, vast areas of spring bulbs, a Japanese garden, a model fruit garden, a vine terrace, a carousel and a neo-medieval castellated folly. It looks down on to a rhododendron garden, expansive drifts of astilbes, a modern rose garden and an area planted with countless of lavender plants. The North Garden, behind the palace, has an ice-house, a *parterre de broderie* and a view up to the adjoining Schlosspark Favorite.

open: All year, daily, 7.30am–8.30pm (or dusk, if earlier)

open: All year, daily, 9am–1pm and 2–5pm. Guided tours only

Further information from:
Schlossgarten Ludwigsburg,
71638-Ludwigsburg
Tel: 07141 910636

Nearby sights of interest:
Schloss Favorite and Schloss Monrepos.

The elegantly restored *parterre de broderie* in the North Garden of Ludwigsburg's Schlossgarten.

Mainau: Insel Mainau

Location: On Bodensee, 7km (4¼ miles) from Konstanz

open: All year, daily, 7am–8pm; (9am–5pm from mid-Oct to mid-Mar)

Further information from:
Insel Mainau, 78465-Mainau
Tel: 07531 3030

Nearby sights of interest:
Take a boat across the Bodensee to Meersburg.

Mainau attracts two million tourists every year. The hard work and resources of 80 gardeners go into maintaining this tropical island paradise north of the Alps.

The 45ha (111 acre) island belonged to the Teutonic knights for many years. Its sides rise to a height of 40m (131ft) above the level of Lake Constance: a tower called the Schwedenturm marks the edge of the plateau where it levels off. The Baroque palace was built in 1740 at the eastern end, with splendid views across the lake. The park was laid out by Grand Duke Friedrich I of Baden when he bought the island in 1853; his descendants still live here. The island is reached from the western end of Lake Constance across an iron bridge 110m (361ft) long. There is also a shuttle service by bus from the ticket office on the mainland to the garden entrance. Only the southern half of the

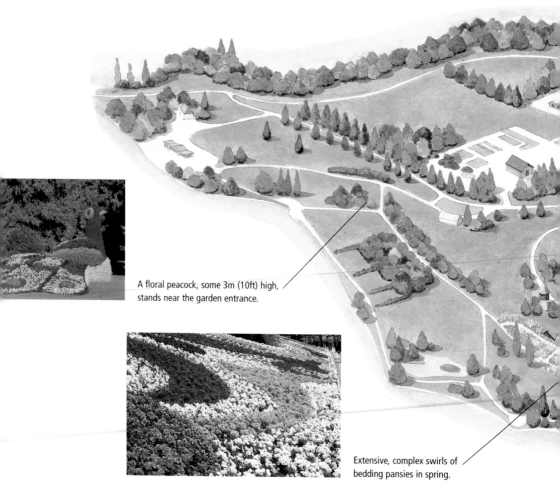

A floral peacock, some 3m (10ft) high, stands near the garden entrance.

Extensive, complex swirls of bedding pansies in spring.

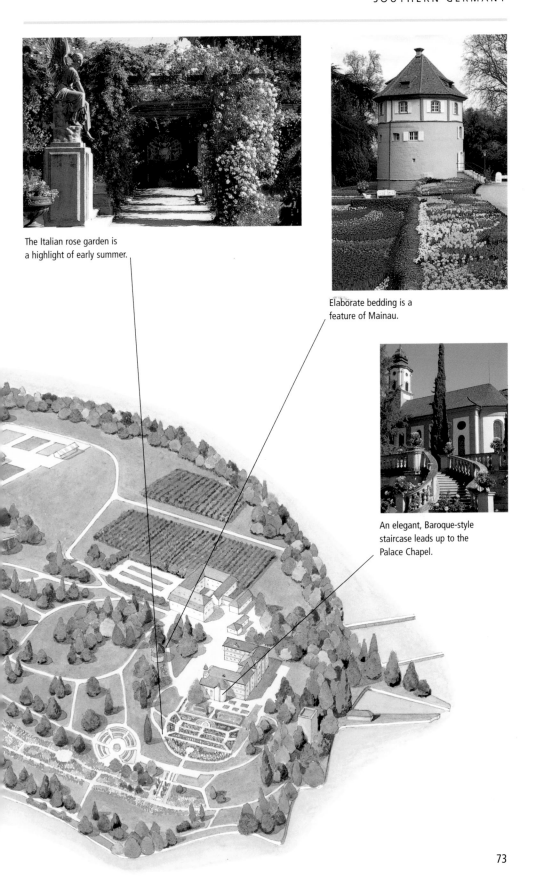

The Italian rose garden is
a highlight of early summer.

Elaborate bedding is a
feature of Mainau.

An elegant, Baroque-style
staircase leads up to the
Palace Chapel.

Neoclassical statues line the rose garden at Insel Mainau.

The rose garden is a mass of glittering colour in early summer.

island can be visited – this is where all the best features can be found: the northern part is a service area for the gardens where some 400,000 bedding plants are raised every year.

The usual circuit of the garden follows the broad lower slopes of the island along its southern side. The first horticultural encounter is with a comic series of huge floral peacocks and ducks standing 3 or 4m (10 or 13ft) high: their plumage is tricked out with bright bedding plants, which are changed according to the season. This leads on to a huge informal garden of shrub roses, planted in 1969 and now the dominant sight in early summer. Many of the roses are grown as unpruned shrubs: the mild climate and good cultivation make for remarkable growth. Mainau has a total of some 30,000 rose bushes.

Beyond are beds for annual display, mainly pansies in spring and dahlias in autumn. The pansies are planted in vast bright abstract swathes. The complex design is best viewed from the terraced gardens above: at lake level the impression is of spectacular colour. Dahlias take over from late summer to mid-autumn and are no less impressive.

Proceed past the floral staircase and the fuchsia garden, then climb the steep hillside to the subtropical terraces, with their wonderful views of the lower garden and across Lake Constance towards its Swiss side. Large palms, cordylines, cacti and many mature greenhouse plants are bedded out here for the summer, together with tender exotics grown as standards including abutilons, heliotrope, lantanas and plumbago. Between these terraces and the palace is the rose garden, laid out in the Italian style by Friedrich I in 1871. It is surrounded by a pergola of climbing roses on three of its sides, while the fourth is the

balustraded garden of the palace itself. The beauty of this garden in early summer is overwhelming: palms and cypresses surround it and increase its exotic allure.

Grand Duke Friedrich was particularly interested in trees. Mainau has a splendid collection of 19th-century conifers in the arboretum and woodland at the top of the island. Several specimens of *Thuya plicata* are more than 40m (131ft) high and one has made thickets where the lower branches have rooted and developed new trunks, which form an extensive "satellite coppice". Among the many deciduous trees are a 42m (138ft) high tulip tree *Liriodendron tulipifera* and a 25m (82ft) Japanese raisin-tree *Hovenia dulcis*: it was planted in 1904 and is now the tallest in Germany. Much of the dense underplanting is with evergreen shrubs, including camellias, osmanthus, pieris and rhododendrons. And the planting continues: part of the private driveway that leads up to the palace has an impressive 200m (656ft) long avenue of metasequoias.

The extensive underplanting of the upper garden with spring bulbs is enchanting. There are millions of them, from crocuses that peep through the lawns around the palace to narcissus which fill the woodland glades. Thick carpets of tulips in the orchards and meadows by the Schwedenturm create successive waves of colour as far as the eye can see. Even in winter the show goes on. In late autumn, the palace terraces are enclosed until spring by a metal and glass structure, and become the Tropenhaus. In its humid houses is a display of *Cyphomandra betacea*, *Musa* species, palms, passion flowers, *Pittosporum tobira*, strelitzias and seasonal bedding plants. New attractions are added at Mainau all the time and throughout the gardens is the sound of birdsong.

Extensive weaving patterns of bedding in late summer.

Munich: Botanic Garden

Location: Entrance from Menzinger Strasse or Park Nymphenburg

open: Daily; Nov to Jan, Apr and Sep, May to Aug, 9am–4pm; Feb, Mar and Oct 9am–5pm. Glasshouses close 30 minutes earlier, and between 11.45am–1pm

Further information from:
Botanischer Garten, Menzinger Strasse 61-65, 80638-München
Tel: 089 17861310

Nearby sights of interest:
Schloss Nymphenburg.

Munich's botanic garden is the most stylish in all Germany and, with more than 14,000 taxa in its 22ha (54 acres), it has one of the best collections of plants in Europe. The central point of its design is the Schmuckhof, an ornamental sunken garden in front of the Botanic Institute's building, where permanent plantings around the formal lily pond are supplemented by seasonal bedding and magnificent displays of horticultural interest.

The whole garden is well designed, intelligently planted and maintained to a very high standard, so that walking around it is a particular pleasure. A keen plantsman could spend all day here, and longer. Its two outstanding features are the rock garden, laid out geographically, and the range of glasshouses, which lead off a central show house. In the "Victoriahaus" are several species and hybrids of *Nymphaea*, including the huge blue-flowered 'Director George T Moore', both species of the giant amazonian water lily, *Victoria cruziana* and *V. amazonica*, and the large flat-leaved *Euryale ferox*. But there many other features to enjoy: a formal rose garden planted with varieties old and new; a rhododendron wood with over 200 cultivars; a lush fern gully; a display of more than 200 protected plants of Germany; a collection of economic plants, which includes some old varieties of cereals; a garden of medicinal plants; systematic beds; a spring garden, overrun early in the year by magnificent sheets of *Crocus tomasinianus*; an arboretum, where trees are planted according to their families; and two typical Bavarian plant communities, one of mesophytic forest and the other of steppe plantings.

The richly-planted Schmuckhof is the focal point of the garden.

Munich: Englischergarten

Location: NE of the city centre

This 370ha (914 acre) civic park was laid out from 1789 onwards
by Friedrich Ludwig von Sckell and the American Count
Rumford for the Elector Karl Theodor (of Schwetzingen fame,
see pp.86–9). The park begins near the palace in the city centre
and stretches for some 5km (3 miles) up the valley of the
River Isar. Since it was laid out purely for public recreation, the
Englischergarten may be regarded as the oldest people's park in
Germany. It is not in any sense attached to a palace or public
building: the landscaping provides its own momentum and
direction. It is beautifully shaped in the English landscape style,
with clumps of beech trees, extending up the valley. Sckell also
used the river to create such features as the broad waterfall. He
was a disciple of the English landscaper Capability Brown, and
an admirer of neoclassicism: the parkland is remarkably free from
sentimental buildings or exotic monuments.

The most harmonious building is the Monopteros, a white
temple on a steep artificial mound which was built by Ludwig I
in 1837. Its Ionic columns support a decorated frieze and cupola.
Less appropriate is the stocky wooden Chinese tower, originally
built in 1789 and five storeys high. It is topped by a copper dome
and sports a pineapple as a finial. The area around the tower has
long been popular for recreation, and has sprouted many cafés
and restaurants. Close to the palace is a modern Japanese tea
garden. It was built at the time of the 1972 Munich Olympics,
and is quite alien to the spirit of the Englischergarten, but
apparently popular with the people of Munich.

Further information from:
Englischer Garten,
80805-München

Nearby sights of interest:
The Residenz at the bottom of
the park.

The elegant Monopteros temple
is the spiritual centre of the
oldest public park in Germany.

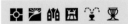

21 # *Munich: Nymphenburg*

Location: 3km (1¾ miles) W of the city centre

open: All year, daily, 8am
to dusk

open: All year, Tue to Sat,
10am–12.30pm and 1.30–4pm

Further information from:
Nymphenburg, 80639-München
Tel: 089 179080

Nearby sights of interest:
The Botanic Garden is adjacent to
the park on its northern edge.

The formal gardens behind
Schloss Nymphenburg are laid
out on a vast scale.

Schloss Nymphenburg is best approached by the Auffahrtsallee,
along the side of the long canal that runs from close to the centre
of Munich right into the *cour d'honneur* of the palace itself. The
central section of the palace is compact and restrained, with its
Corinthian façade and its grey paint, while the surrounding
semicircular courtyard incorporates a series of elegant pavilions
all tricked out in rich yellow. The overriding impression, as one
passes under the porticoes which link the palace to its wings,
is of the sheer size and austerity of the formal gardens, but the
austerity is an illusion because these were originally elaborately
planted and laid out as French parterres. Long lines of bright
bedding around the extreme edges is the most that can be
expected in the way of modern upkeep.

Although the gardens were begun in the 1660s, they were
effectively reworked by Dominique Girard for the Elector
Maximilian, who admired the grand gardens at the palace of
Versailles. It was Maximilian who built
the Pagodenburg tea-house in the
oriental style (1716), and followed it up
with the Badenburg bathing pavilion
(1718) and the Magdalenenklause
hermitage (1725). These handsome
buildings, together with the exquisite
pink-and-white Amalienburg, a hunting
lodge made in 1734 for Maria Amalia
of Austria, the wife of the Elector Karl
Albrecht, are the only garden buildings
which remain of many built during
the 18th century. However, the great
urns and statues found along the edges
of the parterres also date from the
late 18th century.

Friedrich Ludwig von Sckell
landscaped away the formal park in
the early 19th century and created two
natural-looking lakes in the woodland,
the Badenburg and the Pagodenburg.
He left intact the long formal canal
which stretches away into the distance
and provides a fine frame for reflections
of the palace. It is worth walking to the
cascade right at the end of the canal
to appreciate the sheer size and scale
of the garden as it was originally
conceived and laid out.

Munich: Schloss Schleissheim and Schloss Lustheim

Location: Signposted in the village, 14km (8¾ miles) N of Munich

The most remarkable feature of these two princely palaces at Oberschleissheim is the way they face each other straight down a formal garden nearly a kilometre (½ mile) long. Both were built by the Elector Max Emanuel of Bavaria: Lustheim was begun in 1684 and Schleissheim in 1701. Schleissheim is also called the Neues Schloss because it was built in front of the old palace, which still stands, as does the simple, formal garden between them. Schleissheim and Lustheim are linked along the formal axis of a long canal. Enrico Zuccalli was the architect of the gardens, and built the canal in the fashionable Dutch style. It runs for most of the distance between the two palaces, encircles Lustheim (which thus appears to be built on an island) and terminates in a cascade in front of Schloss Schleissheim. It was Dominique Girard who built the cascade in 1724 and completed the gardens, which bear a strong resemblance to his grand formal garden at Augustusburg (see p.108): the long parterres are each rounded off by large circular basins at their corners.

Along the sides of the canal are extensive *bosquets* and the ruins of further formal gardens and rides. The parterres at Schleissheim were remade by Karl Effner in the 1830s, but the garden was never turned into a landscape park. It therefore remains one of the most important early Baroque gardens in Germany, contemporary with Herrenhausen (see pp.124–7).

open: All year, daily, dawn to dusk
open: All year, Tue to Sun, 10am–12.30pm and 1.30–5pm

Further information from:
Schloss Schleissheim,
85764-Oberschleissheim

Nearby sights of interest:
The interiors and paintings of Neues Schloss; Schloss Lustheim – a museum of Meissen porcelain.

The handsome parterres in front of the Schloss are richly-planted with seasonal bedding.

🍴 🛏 ⚱

open: All year, daily, dawn to dusk

Further information from:
Westpark, 80539-München

Nearby sights of interest:
The Theresienwiese: the site of Munich's beery Oktoberfest.

Autumn colour in Westpark's Japanese garden.

Munich: Westpark

Location: At the end of Westendstrasse

Westpark is a modern city park, laid out between 1978 and 1983. It has been beautifully landscaped to disguise its awkward shape. The visitor does not realize that it is exceptionally long and thin, or that its two halves are bisected by a dual carriageway. The main features of horticultural interest are at the western end of the park. Near the small lake sophisticated oriental gardens can be found: a Chinese garden, a Japanese garden, and a Thai garden. Further along is the Bayerischer Waldhaus which is a reconstruction of a 16th-century Bavarian house and garden. The extensive rose garden is largely laid out with modern hybrids, loosely planted in island beds: the seating areas are backed by arbours of climbing roses and clematis.

Westpark is best known for its spacious plantings of alpine and herbaceous plants. These are held together by successive flushes of such flowering plants as geraniums and Michaelmas daisies, planted with a broad brush to intensify their effect. In the eastern part of Westpark the picturesque Sardinian House looks down over the valley towards a lake landscaped with large stones and smooth rocks, which give it a slightly oriental feel. Swamp cypresses flourish along the water's edge and in the lake itself: this planting is particularly pretty when the trees are in new leaf and the nearby bird-cherries in flower.

🖼 👥 🏛

open: All year, daily, dawn to dusk
🏛 **open:** Easter Sat to Sep, Sat, Sun and feast days, 10am–5pm

Further information from:
Patrizierschloss, Neunhof, 90403-Nürnberg

Nearby sights of interest:
Schloss Neunhof is part of the German National Museum. The village is famous for garlic growing.

Nürnberg: Patrizierschloss Neunhof

Location: In the village centre

The castle was built in around 1500 and is dry-moated: its original Baroque garden, made in 1749, is now lost. The modern Baroque garden comes in two parts. The older section lies in front of the castle and was laid out in 1962 to plans from the 17th century. Its box enclosures, already rather overgrown, are cut into simple sections and known as the arabesque parterres. The newer part was begun in 1978 and consists of a dozen grass enclosures hedged to 0.5m (1½ft) by privet. It has copies of four 19th-century comic statues of dwarfs in sandstone: the originals are in the German National Museum in Nuremburg. Pleached plane trees and pretty seasonal bedding complete the picture. The whole ensemble need not detain the visitor for long, but is best visited at a weekend when the castle is open.

Pforzheim: Alpengarten

Location: Signed off U9, 4km (2½ miles) SE of Pforzheim

This famous and extensive rock garden was begun in 1927 in a steep meadow above the River Würm, by an amateur who designed and planted it in accordance with the principles of Karl Förster. Its fame spread quickly and by 1933 it was regularly open to the public. After the war the garden expanded until it reached its present extent of about 2ha (5 acres).

The centrepiece is a magnificent and extensive rock garden, mainly of local sandstone but with areas of imported Swabian limestone for plants that require more porous growing conditions. The range of alpine plants is extensive: the selection of *Primula* species is particularly comprehensive, as are the collections of saxifrages, gentians and lady's slipper orchids. But there is a great variety of different taxa to enjoy here, including slow-growing shrubs, handsome Japanese maples, low-growing rhododendrons and dwarf forms of conifers, some now substantial trees. The paths are lined with many troughs planted with alpines or summer bedding. Beyond the rock garden is a birch wood underplanted with rhododendrons and azaleas whose display reaches its peak in late spring and early summer. The garden also contains an excellent small alpine nursery.

open: Spring to autumn, daily, 8am–7pm

Further information from:
Pforzheimer Alpengarten,
75181-Pforzheim-Würm
Tel: 07231 70590

Nearby sights of interest:
The drive along the River Würm to Tiefenbronn, a famous centre for good food.

Paths through the alpine garden are lined with hundreds of stone troughs.

Rastatt: Schloss Favorite

Location: 4km (2½ miles) SE of Rastatt

open: All year, daily, dawn to dusk

open: All year, Tue to Sun (closes Bank Holidays), 9am–5pm, (closes 4pm Oct to mid-Mar)

Further information from:
Schloss Favorite,
76456-Kuppenheim
Tel: 07222 39363 (Rastatt tourist office)

Nearby sights of interest:
The Schloss; the Spiegelkabinett and Florentiner Zimmer.

Part of the handsome staircase of the palace.

The Schloss was built between 1710 and 1714 as a summer residence for Sibylla Augusta, Margravine of Baden, the widow of Imperial Field Marshall Ludwig Wilhelm, who was known as "Türkenlouis". The approach to the castle is by a double avenue of lime trees in front of a long rectangular lawn, which is all that remains of an extensive formal Baroque garden. Along the sides are galleries where pots of exotic plants, including agapanthus, acacias, hibiscus and oleanders, are put out for the summer.

The palace is now set in a handsome classical park, with some interesting trees and shrubs including *Aesculus parviflora*, *Calycanthus floridus*, limes, planes and tulip trees. It looks out east to a lake with a large island in the middle and beyond to a distant view of the Black Forest hills. The lake is fed by a sinuous watercourse whose source is a long rectangular tank which was once a fishpond. The ensemble adds up to a nice example of the German landscape style which has been embellished over the years with exotic trees.

Rastatt: Schlossgarten and Pagodenburg

Location: In the town centre

The Schlossgarten at Rastatt was originally laid out when the Schloss itself was built at the end of the 17th century, for "Türkenlouis", the Margrave Ludwig Wilhelm of Baden. However, both palace and garden were almost completely destroyed during the Second World War.

The outline of the present garden is based on early 18th-century plans with hedges of hornbeam and yew, avenues and groves of lime trees, crunchy gravel paths and attractive modern formal gardens within the compartments at the sides. These gardens are modern reconstructions in period style and offer such horticultural delights as old roses underplanted with lavender, beds of hydrangeas, pergolas hung with wisteria and a square of flowering cherries: all quite unhistorical, but exceedingly pretty. The main axis is dominated at the eastern end by a handsome modern fountain set in a large octagonal pool.

The Pagodenburg, a stylish and charming garden pavilion, is 150m (492ft) to the south of the Schlossgarten. This elegant Baroque folly was built by Türkenlouis's widow the Margravine Sibylla Augusta in 1722 as a playhouse for her children. The Elector Maximilian of Bavaria sent her copies of the original plans, so that it is an exact replica of the famous Baroque pavilion at Nymphenburg in Munich (see p.78). The garden is laid out on the edge of the town, high above the river and surrounded by formal gardens made in 1955 in the Baroque style. The elegant grass parterres are planted with modern roses, most of them floribundas: below is a new garden, with an arcade of the climbing rose 'New Dawn' along one side. Both this and the Schlossgarten are at their most attractive when the roses flower in early summer.

open: All year, daily, dawn to dusk

open: All year, Tue to Sun, 2–5pm

Further information from:
Schlossgarten and Pagodenburg, 76437-Rastatt
Tel: 07222 22625

Nearby sights of interest:
The palace can be visited: guided tours, daily except Mondays, 9.30am–5pm.

The Pagodenburg at Rastatt is prettily set in a rose garden.

open: All year, daily, dawn to dusk

Further information from:
Sanspareil, 96197-Wonsees

Nearby sights of interest:
The rocky outcrops of the Franken Schweiz.

Sanspareil

Location: S of the A20, about halfway between Bamberg and Bayreuth

The remarkable garden of Sanspareil was made by Margravine Wilhelmina of Baden in the late 1740s. Often considered a prototype of the German romantic movement, Sanspareil owes more to literary allusions than to a love of landscape. The design is based on references to Fénélon's *Les Aventures de Télémaque*, which tells the story of what happened when Télémaque and his tutor Mentor were shipwrecked on Calypso's isle. The natural outcrops and boulders of rock at Sanspareil are left unadorned but take on such names as the Grotto of Calypso, Pan's Seat, the Temple of Aeolius and Vulcan's Cave. The rocks are quite unembellished: all were left as they were found. "Nature herself was the architect" Wilhelmina wrote to her brother Frederick the Great of Prussia in 1745.

Sanspareil straddles a long high ridge planted with beech trees which rustle in the wind. The woodland is perhaps loveliest in late spring, when the leaves begin to grow. There is no under-planting, just the natural flora of old beechwoods. At the end of the circuit is the theatre, deliberately built as a ruin in 1744: its arches enclose the stage where Calypso's nymphs may have danced, while a huge natural rock arch soars over the auditorium. It is remarkable that the Margravine should have had such a refined sensibility at a time when her contemporaries still thought in terms of Baroque artificiality. At the entrance to the garden is a rustic hermitage called the Morgenländischer Bau. The *parterres de broderie* in front have recently been restored.

The awesome "ruined" theatre is the culmination of a visit to Sanspareil.

Schönbusch: Park

Location: 3km (1¾ miles) S-W of Aschaffenburg

Schönbusch is one of the first and finest landscape parks in southern Germany, classical rather than romantic in character. The country house at its centre is pink and small, and sits neatly above the lake. It was designed for the Archbishop-Elector of Mainz in 1778 by J E d'Hérigoyen and acquired by the Kings of Bavaria after the Congress of Vienna. Its meadows are yellow with buttercups in spring and blue with *Salvia pratensis* in summer.

Friedrich Ludwig von Sckell worked on the park from 1785 onwards. Open or wooded parkland, curving paths and rides, and strategically placed glades or clumps of native trees are the essence of his style. The spoil from dredging the lake was used to form two long hummocks (the Berg): they are joined by a soaring arch called the Devil's Bridge, originally made of wood but rebuilt in iron in 1875. The nearby Lighthouse Tower, also originally of wood, was remade in stone in 1867. Best known of all the monuments is the exquisite banqueting house, built for festive occasions in 1792 with a painted sky on the ceiling and murals of the surrounding park so that guests had the illusion of dining outside. Behind the house are the Temple to Friendship and the Philosopher's House, both of which were built between 1799 and 1802 to plans of d'Hérigoyen. There is also a charming memorial to the head gardener Christian Siebold, erected by King Ludwig I, and a long cascade designed by Sckell. But the greatest joy of Schönbusch is to walk the woods and glades, inbibing the beauty of the designed landscape.

open: 15 Mar to 16 Oct, Tue to Sun, 9am–6pm
open: Guided tours from 10am–12.30pm and 1.30–4.30pm. See above for days and months

Further information from:
Schönbusch, 63739-Aschaffenburg
Tel: 06021 395800

Nearby sights of interest:
The collection of Flemish and Dutch old masters in Schloss Johannisberg in Aschaffenburg.

The artificial lake at Schönbusch has acquired a natural appearance.

🔲 🔳 🔲 🏛 🎍 ⛲

open: All year, daily,
8am–8pm (or dusk, if earlier)
open: All year, Tue to Sun,
10am–4pm (closes 5pm Sat, Sun
and Public Holidays)

Further information from:
Schlossgarten,
68723-Schwetzingen
Tel: 06202 4933 (Schwetzingen
tourist office)

Nearby sights of interest:
The Cathedral at Speyer.

29 *Schwetzingen: Schlossgarten*

Location: In the town centre

The Emperor Joseph II travelled from Austria incognito to see its gardens. Voltaire declared that his dying wish was to revisit this "earthly paradise". Schwetzingen is no less compelling today: it is a garden of immense beauty. There is no better place to enjoy the transition from baroque to landscape gardening.

Schwetzingen was the summer residence of the Elector Carl Theodor who succeeded to the Palatinate throne in 1743. His French architect Nicolas de Pigage built long curving extensions on either side of the castle: together they form a semicircle. This inspired the Elector's head gardener to create a circular parterre enclosed on the far side by two curving pergolas of trellis-work. Within this circle he laid out formal gardens, avenues of lime, low hedges and intricately planted flower borders.

The Mosque was Carl Theodor's last and greatest folly at Schwetzingen.

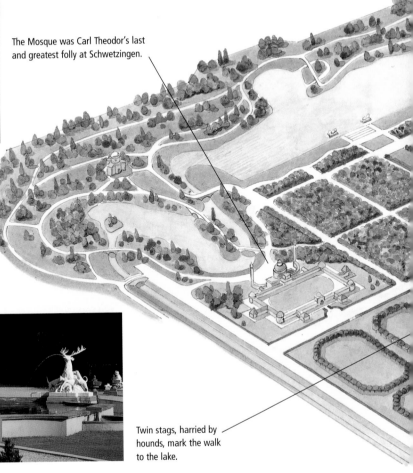

Twin stags, harried by hounds, mark the walk to the lake.

The elegant Chinese bridge is improbably named the Rialto.

The main entrance to the garden is through the arched gateway of the palace itself.

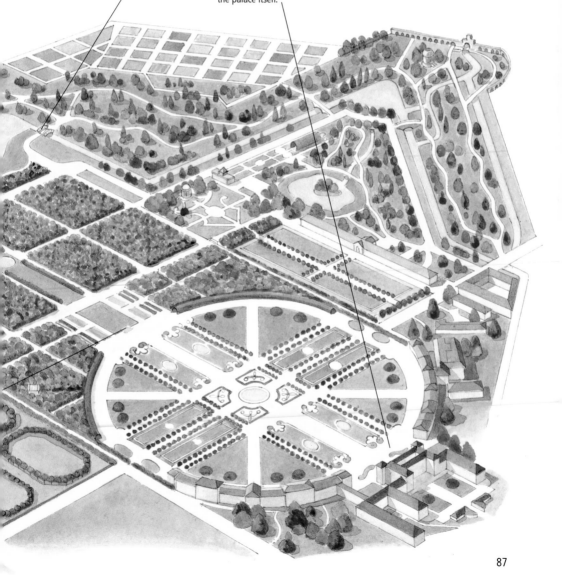

The approach is through the main arched gateway of the palace. The beds within the central parterre are traced with box and filled with colourful bedding. Crab apples grow as small standards, barely 1m (3ft) high. The central fountain has a statue of Arion being rescued by dolphins. When these formal gardens were remade in the 1970s, they were planted as copies of the originals. The result is that Schwetzingen can be seen as it was in the time of the Elector Karl Theodor, as a young garden taking shape.

The central avenue leads on to the Stag Fountain, with handsome sculptures of stags grounded by hounds, and thence to the lake. The woodlands were originally formal groves, intersected by hornbeam avenues. To one side is the Temple of Apollo, high on a terrace which dominates this part of the garden: a statue of the sun-god stands beneath a cupola with a golden sun as its finial. The railings along the edge of the terrace ring the temple with shining golden images of the sun. Beneath them is the Bath House, a place where the Elector could relax with his friends and many mistresses. Its exquisitely decorated interior incorporates an opulent marble bathroom and a tea-room. Nearby is the dramatic Fountain of the Birds: a murderous owl in the central fountain is sprayed with water by birds perched on the top of the encircling trellis-work. Visitors walk under the jets of water which spout from their beaks.

Friedrich Ludwig von Sckell redesigned the outer areas of the garden in the English landscape style in 1776. Fortunately, Sckell had the sense to preserve the formal parterres near the palace. The rectangular pool at the end became the irregularly-shaped lake. Two reclining statues at the water's edge represent the River Rhine and the River Danube. There is a beautiful view back towards the palace from the lakeside, best seen late

A canal runs through the formal garden in front of the orangery.

summer. Tropical water lilies in yellow, blue, violet, pink and white grow alongside Indian lotuses, water hyacinths, *Euryale ferox* and giant Amazonian water lilies. Exotic terraces lead up to a belvedere behind. They are filled with araucarias, cypresses, daturas, hibiscus, olives and orange trees: the palm trees are set out so thickly that one can easily imagine being in the Mediterranean. The conservatories are planted with tropical ferns and economic plants, including everything from cotton bushes and kapok trees to yams, guavas and papaws.

Tübingen: Botanic Garden

Location: In the new university campus site, N of the city centre

The botanic garden at Tübingen dates back to 1675: one of the early rectors of the university was Leonhart Fuchs, for whom the genus *Fuchsia* was named. The garden has been on its present site since the 1960s. It extends to 10ha (25 acres) on a steep hillside north of the city and has about 12,000 taxa in its living collections. The first area to impress the visitor is a rock garden.

The whole garden has been beautifully landscaped around a curving valley, whose sides are planted with systematic beds, which include an exposition of Swabian plants, as well as geological and ecological collections. The paths down the hillside and the stream at the bottom are planted with ornamentals, including rhododendrons and aquatic plants. The splendid spacious tropical house is some 12m (39ft) high, giving room for such plants as *Anamirta paniculata* and *Bambusa arundinacea* to reach an impressive height. Nearby are two cactus houses with an excellent display of plants from South Africa (the species of *Lithops* are especially interesting), the Canary islands and other dry parts of the world.

The arboretum lies on the hillside across the road above the botanic garden and contains about 2,000 taxa. Although principally used for scientific research, attention has been paid to ornamental effects – deciduous species and hybrids of *Magnolia* line the paths and Japanese maples are grouped for their autumn colour. As the arboretum is so young, it is interesting to see how quickly things have grown, in particular the willows, birches, limes and poplars. Enthusiasts for trees and shrubs will find this collection fascinating, whatever the time of the year.

open: All year, Mon to Fri, 7.30am–4.45pm. Sat, Sun and Public Holidays, opens 8am

Further information from:
Botanischer Garten der Universität, Hartmeyerstr. 123, 72076-Tübingen
Tel: 07071 292609

Nearby sights of interest:
The old city of Tübingen: the Markt and the Holzmarkt are particularly charming.

Ornamental plantings line the path to the splendid glasshouses.

open: All year, daily, dawn to dusk
open: All year, daily, 9am–12 noon, 1–5pm

Further information from:
Hofgarten, 97209-Veitshöchheim

Nearby sights of interest:
Würzburg.

Veitshöchheim: Hofgarten

Location: In the town centre

Veitshöchheim is the most famous rococo garden in Germany. The design evolved from 1700 onwards, changing as it developed, so that ideas and fashions from different periods are fused together in one spectacular work of art. Many Prince-Bishops of Würzburg contributed to it, but it was Adam Friedrich von Seinsheim who decorated it with statues in such as way as to bind the older baroque garden with his own rococo additions.

Each successive garden room leads to new delights in the fascinating layout. Sometimes it is difficult to keep a sense of direction among the high hornbeam hedges and alleys of pleached limes. And there are secret gardens within the groves, some planted with modern roses.

The lower section of the Hofgarten centres on the Pegasus Fountain in the Grosser See: statues of Apollo and the nine Muses on Mount Parnassus attend a huge-winged horse rearing up to fly heavenwards. The number and variety of the Ferdinand Dietz's enchanting statues are the essence of Veitshöchheim. There is no limit to their invention and wit. In the woodland part are two bizarre *chinois* baldachinos, their cupolas supported by sculpted palm trees, topped by enormous pineapples. Under the belvedere in the south-east corner is an enchanting animal grotto.

This *trompe l'oeil* vista between two pavilions is typical of Veitshöchheim's sense of fun.

Weikersheim: Schlossgarten

Location: In the town centre

Schlossgarten Weikersheim is one of the most exuberant and fanciful gardens in Germany. This Baroque pleasure garden was the work of Graf Carl Ludwig von Hohenlohe in the early 18th century. The approach is impressive: it passes through an arch beneath the Renaissance castle, then over a bridge across the old moat and between golden gates hung on pinnacled pillars. Along the wall of the moat, well outside the formal garden, is a row of 16 extraordinary dwarfs and dwarfesses: these richly humorous caricatures were carved by J J Sommer and his sons between 1708 and 1725.

The huge central parterre is a quincunx, originally laid out in 1708 and still lined on either side with statues of nymphs, gods and heroes. The bedding-out is extensive, but confined to narrow strips along the edge and the entire design is tricked out with trees and shrubs in tubs and Versailles cases – clipped box, agapanthus, oleanders, orange trees and pomegranates. A giant statue of Hercules struggling with the Hydra is the centrepiece of the pool in the middle but the main axis runs through it and terminates dramatically in large twin orangeries, whose roofs bristle with statues. The stately orangeries extend across the width of the formal garden, and block off an extensive view of the surrounding countryside, save for a semicircular recess between them which opens up to give a charming vista of the hilly Tauber Valley. This focal point sports a statue of Graf Carl Ludwig von Hohenlohe himself, flanked by no lesser persons than Caesar Augustus, Cyrus, Alexander the Great and Nimrod. There is nothing to match the sheer bravura of Weikersheim's Baroque invention.

open: All year, daily, 8.30am–6pm
open: Daily: Apr to Oct, 8.30am–6pm; Nov to Mar, 10am to 12 noon and 2–4pm

Further information from:
Schloss Weikersheim,
97990-Weikersheim
Tel: Weikersheim tourist office
07934 7272

Nearby sights of interest:
The Teutonic Knights had their HQ at the enormous Deutschordensschloss at Bad Mergentheim.

Wiekersheim, Schlossgarten: the central quincunx is an extrovert design.

open: Mar to Oct, Tue to Sun, 10am–7pm

Further information from:
Schau- und Sichtungsgarten Hermannshof, 69469-Weinheim-an-der-Bergstrasse

Nearby sights of interest:
The old town centre of Weinheim.

37 *Weinheim: Hermannshof*

Location: In the town centre

Hermannshof is a show garden and trial-ground for perennial plants and one of the most instructive gardens in Germany. It complements the experimental work at Weihenstephan and fulfils three aims. The first is to discover which plants will co-exist in given growing conditions so that no variety dominates all the others. The second aim is to create plant combinations which look well together because of their harmonies and contrasts of colour or form. The third purpose is to establish attractive and permanent plantings which will flourish with little maintenance but offer interest and colour over a long period. The principles of modern German planting are here scaled down and applied to small private gardens.

There are seven habitats within the garden that reproduce common growing conditions: woodland, woodland edge, steppe, rocky ground, water's edge, water, and ordinary garden borders. Individual areas within these communities create their greatest effects at different times of the year. The intention is to imitate nature and often the same plant is repeated throughout a large grouping to give the impression of self-seeding.

Weinheim's mild climate supports a wide range of plants and there are some 2,000 cultivars of herbaceous plants alone. Students of plants and gardens should visit Hermannshof, not just to see and copy the good combinations, but to ponder over the underlying principles.

Experimental plantings combine the highest achievements of science and art at Weinheim.

Weinheim: Schlosspark and Exotenwald

Location: In the old town centre

open: All year, daily, 7am–10pm

Further information from:
Schlosspark and Exotenwald, 69469-Weinheim-an-der-Bergstrasse

Nearby sights of interest:
Mannheim and Heidelberg.

The Schloss at Weinheim is now the town hall, and the large bush of *Poncirus trifoliata* against its wall gives a clue to the history of the whole estate, for both the Schlosspark and the Exotenwald were systematically planted with exotic plants in the late 19th century. The Berckheim family, who owned the estate, used the park and created the arboretum to test the adaptability of new species to this mild corner of Baden-Württemberg.

The Schlosspark was first laid out in the 1790s in the English style by Friedrich Ludwig von Sckell. A classic glade of grass sweeps up to a belvedere and the neo-Byzantine mausoleum of the Berckheims at the top of the garden. Shady walks, handsome conifers, rhododendrons and excellent seasonal bedding intensify the romantic character of the park.

In 1860 Christian Freiherr von Berckheim started to plant the 60ha (148 acres) which are now the Exotenwald, in the valley below the present Schlosspark. Only a handful of the trees are rare – they total some 80 taxa – but they have often been planted in significant groups, notably a large number of 19th-century *Sequoiadendron giganteum* and a modern planting of *Picea omorika*. There are several good walks around the Exotenwald: the shortest recommended by the guide published by the Forestry Ministry is 2.4km (1½ miles) long.

Summer bedding is attractively maintained in the Schlosspark at Weinheim.

39 *Würzburg: Botanic Garden*

Location: SE of the city near Autobahn E5/A3 exit Würzburg-Heidingsfeld

open: All year, daily, 8am–6pm (closes 4pm Oct to Mar).

Further information from:
Botanischer Garten der Universität, Mittl. Dallenbergweg 64a, 97082-Würzburg
Tel: 0931 8886240

Nearby sights of interest:
Sights in the city.

The botanical institute was founded in 1696, but this imaginative modern 8ha (20 acre) garden was made during the 1960s. Near the entrance are a model vegetable garden, a wildflower garden, a cottage garden, an ornamental plant garden and a physic garden.

The outstanding feature of Würzburg's botanic garden is the large area devoted to geographical and habitat groupings, some 20 of them, including steppe plants of Europe, meadow plants of Asia Minor, and Mediterranean rock plants from the Near East. The rock garden has a wall of naturalized aubrietas, *Campanula garganica* and *C. portenschlagiana*. The arboretum is laid out as a woodland: here too, many underplantings have naturalized, including columbines, hellebores and *Melittis melissiphyllum*. Other areas are devoted to diverse woodland habitats, such as German beechwoods, Balkan hornbeam woods and alpine black pine forests. Then there are the steppe communities: even the flat roof of a faculty building has been planted as a gravel garden.

The institute has 15 glasshouses, including houses for tropical water plants, alpines, Mediterranean plants, and cacti and succulents of South Africa and North America. The garden also has a collection of Japanese plants made to commemorate Philipp von Siebold (1796–1866), a native of Würzburg.

Exotic plants have naturalized throughout the rock garden.

40 *Würzburg: Hofgarten*

Location: In the city centre

open: All year, daily, dawn to dusk
open: All year, Tue to Sun, 9am–5pm (10am–4pm Nov to Mar)

Further information from:
Hofgarten, 97070-Würzburg
Tel: 0931 37436 (Würzburg tourist office)

Nearby sights of interest:
The Residenz is a must: designed by Balthasar Neumann with ceilings by Tiepolo (the largest fresco in the world).

The garden attached to the Bishops' Residence in Würzburg has one of the most splendid baroque layouts of the 18th century. It comes in two parts, each attached to one of the palace's façades. The smaller one lies to the south of the palace and although it is the lesser of the two gardens, it is still amazingly grand. Highlights include conical yews around a central pond, statues of Europa and the Rape of Proserpina, roses, and excellent bedding plants planted in stripes of colour.

The main garden to the east of the palace was given its definitive form during the reign of Prince-Bishop Adam Friedrich von Seinsheim (1757–79). In the 19th century it was overlaid with a landscape design and planted with exotic trees and shrubs. By 1830 it had over 2,500 different taxa and the contents of the garden were more highly valued than its design.

Since World War II it has been restored to its 18th-century form, but with a big bold bed of modern roses immediately outside the palace. There are arches of laburnum and mulberry, statues of dwarfs, urns planted with fuchsias, roses or clipped ivy trained against the walls, shady seats, arcades of thuya backed by sweet-scented shrubs, and rich bedding. The focal point at the top of the terracing is a huge purple beech, a poor replacement for the original Baroque pavilion but a mighty specimen.

Würzburg: Okogarten

Location: On the corner of Luitpoldstrasse and Dreikronenstrasse

The Okogarten has two parts: one is the natural garden set around the Okohaus, which was built for the Landesgartenschau in 1990, while the other is an extensive herbaceous garden in the new German style. Both are maintained organically.

A stream runs the length of the gardens from a spectacular fountain at the top to a peaceful pool at the bottom. Halfway down is a modern cottage garden in the form of a quincunx around a well-head. Here a rustic mixture of vegetables and ornamental plants is grown. Nearby are a herb garden and areas given to the making of composts and mulches. A small orchard is planted with a selection of fruit and nut trees.

The herbaceous plantings at the bottom of the garden are excellent examples of natural planting in semi-wild drifts. Clump-making plants are repeated across a wide area to increase their impact and to unify the ensemble. They are punctuated by individual spiky plants, such as *Asphodeline lutea*. The garden exemplifies the fashion for unnatural nature and disorderly order.

open: All year, daily, 8am to dusk

open: All year, Tue and Thu, 12 noon to 4pm; Wed, 9am–1pm

Further information from:
Okogarten, Luitpoldstrasse 7a, 97082-Würzburg
Tel: 0931 43972

Nearby sights of interest:
The Festung Marienberg, which houses the Mainfränkisches Museum.

The Okogarten is approached through this magnificent natural planting of perennials.

Key to gardens

1 Anholt: **Wasserburg**
2 Bielefeld: **Botanic Garden**
3 Bonn: **Botanic Garden**
4 Bremen: **Rhododendron Park and Botanic Garden**
5 Brühl: **Schloss Augustusburg**
6 Cologne: **Arboretum**
7 Cologne: **Botanic Garden**
8 Darmstadt: **Botanic Garden**
9 Darmstadt: **Mathildenhöhe**
10 Darmstadt: **Prinz-Georgs-Garten**
11 Dortmund: **Rombergpark**
12 Dortmund: **Westfalenpark**
13 Düsseldorf: **Botanic Garden**
14 Düsseldorf: **Nordpark**
15 Düsseldorf: **Schloss Benrath**
16 Essen: **Grugapark**
17 Essen: **Villa Hügel**
18 Frankfurt: **Palmengarten**
19 Glücksburg: **Jensen Rose Garden**
20 Göttingen: **Old and New Botanic Gardens**
21 Hamburg: **Botanic Garden**
22 Hamburg: **Planten un Blomen**
23 Hanau: **Wilhelmsbad**
24 Hanover: **Botanic Garden**
25 Hanover: **Herrenhausen**
26 Kassel: **Insel Siebenbergen**
27 Kassel: **Karlsaue**
28 Kassel: **Wilhemshöhe**
29 Kassel: **Schloss Wilhelmstal**
30 Kiel: **Botanic Garden**
31 Krefeld: **Botanic Garden**
32 Lütetsburg: **Schlosspark**
33 Münster: **Botanic Garden**
34 Nordkirchen: **Schlossgarten**
35 Oldenburg: **Botanic Garden**
36 Oldenburg: **Schlossgarten**
37 Sögel: **Schloss Clemenswerth**
38 Uetersen: **Rose Garden**
39 Weilburg: **Schlossgarten**
40 Wuppertal: **Botanic Garden**
41 Zweibrücken: **Europas Rose Garden**

Key

— Motorways
— Principal trunk highways
(3) Gardens
● Major towns and cities
• Towns

Garden tours

— Western tour: 15, 13, 14, 16, 17, 40
— Frankfurt tour: 18, 23, 10, 8, 9

Western & Northern Germany

Lübeck

eburg

elzen

Volfsburg

unschweig
er

Western and northern Germany look to Britain and the Netherlands for their cultural inspiration and trading partners. Throughout the 18th and 19th century Hanover was linked to the kings of England, while such parts as East Friesland were closer to the Low Countries than to imperial Germany. To this day such Catholic enclaves as Rheinland-Pfalz and the Münsterland are different in character, altogether more easy-going than Protestant Lower Saxony. The charm of Schloss Benrath at Düsseldorf (see p.115) has no counterpart among the palaces and gardens of the Protestant princes. Benrath was a northern outpost of the lands attached to the Palatinate. The northernmost territories of the Elector Clemens August of Cologne included the Baroque gardens at Clemenswerth (see p.136).

Minor princes have also left their monuments across the flat northern plains: the historic

The Baroque Teehaus at Anholt looks over a modern parterre.

gardens at Nordkirchen and Anholt are attached to Wasserburgs – the red-bricked castles and castellated palaces surrounded by at least one geometrical moat, preferably two. But the greatest historic gardens in these regions were made by the princes of Hanover and Kassel. Herrenhausen (see pp.124–7) is not only one of the largest Baroque gardens in northern Europe, it is also one of the oldest. The work of Landgrave Karl at Kassel also dates from the early years of the 18th century: one can but wonder at the energy and riches displayed by the Landgraves of Kassel and by their descendant the Elector Wilhelm I. But this region also incorporates some of the greatest cities of the Hansa League with their tradition of independence. Hamburg is perhaps the outstanding example: here there are no grand historic parks and palaces, but a tradition of academic learning and civic gardening instead.

Western Germany also encompasses the Rühr. It is a land of botanic collections and grand civic gardens. Many botanic gardens are 19th-century foundations, a product of the reordering of Germany after the Congress of Vienna. They are industrial symbols of the value of empirical learning and statements of a city's own importance. It follows that this is also the best part of Germany for flower gardens. Here public gardens and parks reach their most sophisticated development: the 19th-century wonders of Palmengarten at Frankfurt (see p.117) have inspired the more populist Westfalenpark in Dortmund (see p.113), Nordpark in Düsseldorf (see p.115), Grugapark in Essen (see p.116), and Planten un Blomen in Hamburg (see p.121). These modern gardens are also the leading exponents of the new style of German planting, which is particularly appropriate not only to public parks

The new Rhododendron Garden found at Palmengarten in Frankfurt.

but also to botanic gardens where it serves to illustrate how different ecologies actually develop in the wild. The best examples of the genre may be found at Grugapark in Essen and Westfalenpark in Dortmund.

Japanese gardens are also seen in many public parks in this part of the country, often maintained by a local group of enthusiasts for Japanese forms. Düsseldorf's Nordpark is one of the best: perhaps its most striking feature is a grove of pine trees 3–4m (10–13ft) high but trained in the bonsai style. But the largest Japanese garden in Europe is at Planten un Blomen in Hamburg.

The charming statue of Bacchus at Schloss Benrath.

The north and west of Germany have a milder climate than the east and south. In East Friesland, Bremen and Schleswig-Holstein, for instance, it is lushly temperate. This is the land of rhododendrons, which find the sandy soils and cool climates so strongly to their tastes. Go in late spring, when the rhododendrons are at their peak and be sure to visit the Rhododendron park at Bremen (see p.107). From early summer onwards, roses too are a great feature of German gardens in the north and west. As well as the national collection at Westfalenpark in

Prinz-Georgs-Garten in Darmstadt: the sundial in the foreground dates from 1750.

Dortmund, there are fine public parks devoted to roses from Uetersen in the north (see p.137) to Zweibrücken in the south west (see p.139). And the flowers and gardens of this region are supplied by the best nurseries in Germany. The centre of the horticultural industry – especially rhododendron nurseries – is north of Oldenburg, and impressive to visit. However, the best rose nurseries are in Schleswig-Holstein, and friendly rivalry between such growers as Tantau and Kordes was responsible for the founding of the rose garden at Uetersen in the 1930s.

Anholt: Wasserburg

open: 15 Mar to 15 Oct, Tue to Sun, 10am–6pm

open: As above

Further information from:
Wasserburg Anholt,
46419-Isselburg
Tel: 02874 45353

Nearby sights of interest:
Anholt is very close to the Dutch border.

Location: In the village

The handsome red-brick Wasserschloss at Anholt bristles with turrets. Waterlilies and swans inhabit its moat, and around it lies one of the most impressive privately owned gardens in Germany, maintained to a high standard and completely restored since 1945. On the north side is a modern parterre designed around the letter S (for the Salm family who own the Schloss), tricked out in box with a yew surround. A bridge leads across the moat to a Dutch island garden dating from c1700 but given a Baroque layout in 1966, when it was planted as a modern rose garden with Kordes roses (see p.137). The sandstone sculptures (c1710) include allegorical figures and vases carved with the four seasons: look out for a particularly charming statue of Bacchus, the god of wine. A rustic bridge leads over to the Baroque tea-house, fronted by a little modern parterre. Under an arbour of weeping elm is the entrance to the maze, a reconstruction of the original 18th-century layout, made in 1987 of thuja hedges that are clipped to a height of 2m (6½ft). Fortunately there is an observation platform nearby where anxious parents can shout instructions to their lost children – or vice-versa.

Beyond the outer moat lies the extensive landscape park, exquisitely laid out by the Englishman Edward Milner c1860. The park has an excellent collection of trees, not enough for it to be called an arboretum (not least because plantings are subordinate to the landscape) but offering much to interest the keen dendrologist. It is particularly rewarding in late spring when the rhododendrons are in flower.

A large "S", for the Salm family, forms the centre of this parterre.

Bielefeld: Botanic Garden

Location: Take the Hallerweg Bridge over Ostwestfalen Damm and follow the signs

Bielefeld shows how well a botanic garden can flourish as a public pleasure garden, while yet instructing its visitors in matters botanical. Its opening piece is a spectacular essay in colourful display: the visitor walks up from the entrance, turns a corner and looks up to an enchanting timber-framed cottage at the end of a long lawn, set among brilliant bedding. Founded in 1912, the garden is on the edge of the town and runs up into the Teutoburger Forest. It boasts a fine collection of azaleas, drifts of candelabra primulas, an excellent rock garden, a grove of Japanese maples, a heather garden, and a garden of shade-loving plants. Among its trees are a good specimen of *Cunninghamia lanceolata* and *Quercus macranthera*. The systematic beds support a small collection of medicinal and culinary herbs, but one of the most interesting areas is a small garden devoted to the plants of Nordrhein-Westfalen that are threatened in the wild. The garden is well labelled and kept to a high standard, a credit to Bielefeld.

open: All year, daily, dawn to dusk

Further information from:
Botanischer Garten, Am Kahlenberg 16, 33602-Bielefeld
Tel: 0521 513178

Nearby sights of interest:
The old castle of Sparrenburg.

The horticultural effects at Bielefeld Botanic Garden are one of its charms.

Bonn: Botanic Garden

Location: Entrance in Meckenheimer Allee

open: Apr to Sep, daily, 9am–6pm (opens 1pm Sun and Public Holidays); Oct to Mar, Mon to Fri, 9am–4pm

Further information from:
Botanischer Garten der Universität, Meckenheimer Allee 171, 53115-Bonn
Tel: 0228 732259

Nearby sights of interest:
Robert Schumann's house is at nearby Sebastianstrasse 182, and has a fine collection of memorabilia associated with the composer's last years.

This charming historic garden has an excellent collection of plants. Its 6.5ha (16 acres) contain some 8,000 taxa, of which 5,000 grow in the fully automated and computerized glasshouses. At its centre is the beautiful Baroque Schloss Clemensruh. It was built in 1746 by Clemens August, the grandest of all the Electors of Cologne. Bonn claims to benefit from a mild Atlantic climate, which explains why such comparatively tender trees as the monkey puzzle (*Araucaria araucana*) and the nutmeg yew (*Torreya nucifera*) have grown into tall specimens.

The systematic beds are extensive but the garden also has geographical beds, where the flora of a particular part of the world is grown together as might be expected in the wild. There are a fine rock garden, a lake, and a shade house. Many of the tender species from Australia and subtropical parts of the world are put out in their pots during the warmer months. To one side of the Schloss is a formal rose garden, with huge specimens of *Banksia serrata* in tubs in summer.

The glasshouses include a palm house, tropical fern house, succulent house, Mediterranean house, two orchid houses, a "Victoriahaus" and a house for insectivorous plants. The mangrove house is best known for the regular flowering of the plant with the largest inflorescence in the entire plant kingdom – *Amorphophallus titanum*.

Schloss Clemensruh framed by tall plants of *Banksia serrata* in Bonn's Botanic Garden.

Bremen: Rhododendron Park and Botanic Garden

Location: Signposted at the eastern end of the city

open: All year, daily, 7.30am to dusk. Glasshouses open: 20 Mar to 30 Apr, daily, 7.30am to dusk

Further information from:
Botanischer Garten und Rhododendron Park, 28359-Bremen
Tel: 0421 3613025

Nearby sights of interest:
The Marktplatz in Bremen is worth seeing: the Rathaus and Dom contrast with the Haus der Bürgerschaft.

This beautiful and instructive garden has the largest collection of rhododendrons in mainland Europe. It was begun in 1936 by the newly founded German Rhododendron Society and officially opened in 1937. It owes its position to the mild damp climate of north-west Germany and its proximity to the great rhododendron nurseries of the Rastede area. The park has 700 of the world's 1,000 rhododendron species within its 36ha (89 acres), as well as hybrids from around the world. It is a place of pure enchantment when all the species and hybrids in their myriad colours reach a peak in late spring or early summer.

The rhododendrons are spaciously planted in light natural woodland. The landscaping is superb, with island beds within the grassy glades so that the composition constantly changes. It is also beautifully planted: larger specimens are allowed to build up the mass and create the structure. Beds of low-growing varieties serve as a foreground to huge banks of colour beyond. All the plants are clearly labelled. The largest glasshouse is dedicated to tropical and subtropical species and another has a collection of Vireya rhododendrons from New Guinea.

The Rhododendron Park also incorporates Bremen's Botanic Garden, which is very different in character. It is laid out with both modern and formal systematic beds, and concentrates to some extent upon woodlanders. An area is devoted to indigenous flora and there is also a large alpine garden.

Banks of azaleas reflected in the lakes in late spring.

open: All year, daily, dawn to dusk

open: Feb to Nov, Tue to Sun, 9am to 12 noon and 1.30–4pm

Further information from:
Schloss Brühl (Augustusburg),
50321-Brühl
Tel: 02232 79345 (Brühl tourist office)

Nearby sights of interest:
The grand Baroque palace which has a ceremonial staircase designed by Balthasar Neumann; Phantasialand.

Brühl: Schloss Augustusburg

Location: Well-signposted from the town centre and the motorway

Augustusburg was built in 1725 by Clemens August, a clerical pluralist who succeeded his uncle as Archbishop and Elector of Cologne in 1723 at the age of 23. The grandeur of the palace is matched by the grandeur of the gardens, which were laid out by Dominique Girard between 1727 and 1728. Girard made the complex parterre with its four round pools into the focal point of his design. The box *broderies* are elaborately cut and filled with coloured gravels and bedding plants. Most of the statues and ornaments are now lost, but the modern reconstruction makes it possible to enjoy the layout as it existed in the 18th century. The parterre runs up to an extensive waterpiece, which is fed by a long shallow water staircase from a large circular pool at the end. The main avenue then continues along a straight ride down an avenue through a beech plantation into the distance, ending – it appears – in infinity.

Both the palace and gardens suffered from Napoleon's abolition of the clerical Electors. They were eventually rescued from ruin by the intervention of King Frederick William IV of Prussia who commissioned Peter Joseph Lenné in 1842 to restore Girard's formal garden and enhance it by adding a picturesque landscape layout in the woods beyond. To the side of the main garden is a series of reconstructions, historically inexact but very pretty in summer. They include a *jardin secret* in the 18th-century style, and a modern rose garden: double-flowered pomegranates are among the many tender plants put out for the summer.

The extensive and intricate parterres at Schloss Augustusburg have recently been restored.

Cologne: Arboretum

Location: Signposted on the road from Köln-Sud to Rodenkirchen

open: All year, daily, 9am–8pm (closes 6pm Mar, Sep and Oct, and 4pm Nov to Feb)

The Forstbotanischer Garten at Rodenkirchen is a woodland garden within a young 25ha (62 acre) arboretum. It was begun in 1963 and densely planted, so that it already gives the impression of being mature and even overgrown. The main entrance ride is planted with magnolias and *Cornus florida*, underplanted with azaleas. It leads to azalea walks, a heather garden, collections of conifers, and avenues planted with fine specimen trees.

The arboretum is laid out on a grid, but other parts of the garden have rather more irregular shapes, most notably a sunken rhododendron garden which has been well landscaped with curving paths through it. It is immaculately maintained: its beds are tidy and its paths swept clean. The rhododendron collection is one of the largest in Germany and, though the garden offers a wide variety of woodland shrubs, it is best seen in spring when the rhododendrons are in flower. Do not miss the young blocks of *Sequoiadendron giganteum*, which may some day be one of the great dendrological sights of Germany.

Further information from:
Forstbotanischer Garten,
Köln-Rodenkirchen
Tel: 0421 3613025

Nearby sights of interest:
Bonn, the "small town" which was Germany's capital for more than 50 years.

A woodland walk, lined with ferns and rhododendrons, in Cologne's Forstbotanischer Garten.

Cologne: Botanic Garden

Location: Off Stammheimerstrasse, opposite the zoo

open: All year, daily,
8am–9pm (or dusk, if earlier)

Further information from:
Flora und Botanischer Garten,
50667-Köln
Tel: 02232 79345

Nearby sights of interest:
The city centre, especially the cathedral, the Wallraf-Richartz/Ludwig Museum, the Römisch-Germanisches Museum and the many fine churches.

Cologne's Botanic Garden is rich in horticultural plants and beautiful plantings.

This 11.5ha (28 acre) garden offers the perfect balance between botany and horticulture, scientific display and public amenity. It was originally laid out in the 1860s as a public park by Peter Joseph Lenné. Among the oldest and largest trees that date from his plantings are a copper beech, *Fagus sylvatica* Atropurpurea Group, with a trunk some 6.65m (22ft) in diameter, and a huge Caucasian wingnut, *Pterocarya fraxinifolia*. It was modified in 1914 to incorporate a new botanic garden for Cologne, whose original one had disappeared under the Hauptbahnhof. The garden has some 10,000 taxa in its collection and the flowing design conveys the visitor through the many different areas.

The main entrance leads into a formal garden in a modern adaptation of the Baroque style, where bedding plants are used to create sumptuous displays. To the left is an extensive heath garden of dwarf conifers and heathers, which leads past the fern garden to the systematic beds. But there are also display beds for genera of horticultural importance, such as composites, grasses, labiates, lilies, magnolias, maples, and *Papaveraceae*, integrated into the landscaping throughout the garden.

Separate areas are dedicated to dune flora, woodland plants, azaleas, shade-loving plants, primulas, Mediterranean plants, rhododendrons, herbs, fuchsias, water plants and alpines, and there is also a beautiful winding iris garden. The glasshouses include two tropical houses, and a cacti and succulent house.

8 *Darmstadt: Botanic Garden*

Location: On the eastern edge of the town

Darmstadt's 4.5ha (11 acre) botanic garden has been on its present site since 1874 and has a traditional 19th-century layout. This includes a selection of magnificent mature conifers which in some places have tended to crowd out the underplantings. Nevertheless, it is a garden of great charm.

Among the many interesting plants are the rare native *Sorbus* x *thuringiaca* and a huge, 13m (43ft) high specimen of *Rhamnus cathartica*. There is also a fine *R. imeretina* from the Caucasus, whose large leaves make it the most impressive of all the buckthorns. As well as the usual systematic beds, the garden has good collections of grasses, beds of iris and daylilies, an interesting *Rosaceae* section, an attractive small heather garden, fine enkianthus and azaleas, tanks for aquatics, and a stream where the purple parasite *Lathraea clandestina* has naturalized upon the roots of willows and poplars. Many tropical plants are put out for the summer months, including acacias, banksias, eucalyptus, ferns, palms, and the handsome *Isoplexis canariensis* from Tenerife. One of the many unusual plants in the glasshouses is *Welwitschia mirabilis*, the "botanical dinosaur" from the coasts of Namibia and Angola.

open: All year, daily, 7.30am–7.30pm (closes 4pm Oct to Apr, 12 noon Sun and Public Holidays)

Further information from:
Botanischer Garten der Techn. Hochschule, Schnittspahnstr. 5, 64287-Darmstadt
Tel:06151 163502

Nearby sights of interest:
The Jugendstil monuments in the town centre.

Systematic beds in the sandy soil of Darmstadt's Botanic Garden.

9 *Darmstadt: Mathildenhöhe*

Location: E of the town centre

Grand Duke Ernst-Ludwig of Hesse-Darmstadt established an artists' colony here and encouraged its members to create works of art for the benefit of the town. As well as a Russian Orthodox church (1899), the Art Nouveau wedding tower (1908), and the artists' houses, there is a landscaped park with intriguing garden buildings. But the centrepiece is a startlingly inventive garden of sculpture, which draws on classical, Egyptian, Assyrian, and Hittite elements and is dominated by Bernard Hoetger pieces. The sculptures are arranged around a plantation of trained planes, regularly planted in lines and pollarded, which dates from the early 19th century. Visitors should also walk along Olbrichweg and see the rose garden, the lion gate, and the mausoleum of the Dukes of Hesse-Darmstadt.

open: All year, daily, dawn to dusk

Further information from:
Mathildenhöhe, 64283-Darmstadt

Nearby sights of interest:
The Russian cathedral and the Art Nouveau Exhibition Hall.

open: All year, daily, dawn to dusk

Further information from:
Prinz-Georgs-Garten,
64283-Darmstadt
Tel: 06151 163502

Nearby sights of interest:
The Porcelain Museum has a large collection of Imperial Russian porcelain as well as local work.

Prinz-Georgs-Garten is designed in formal 18th-century style.

Darmstadt: Prinz-Georgs-Garten

Location: Just N of the city centre, E of the Herrengarten

This exceptionally pretty formal garden was originally laid out as a Rococo pleasure garden in 1748 and last remade in 1991. It is "L"-shaped, with small palaces at its two ends and overlapping parterres between. The four-square garden in front of the Prinz-Georg-Palais centres on a small fountain in a circular pool. The longer, narrower parterre in front of the Prettlacksches Gartenhaus (1711) has a central axis lined with yew topiary, as well as a fountain and an Italian wellhead. But the pleasure of this garden lies as much in its luxuriant bedding as its design, and this is complemented by pleached peach and apple trees, and narrow box hedges. It is exactly the sort of historical pastiche at which German garden designers excel and, although it actually extends to 1.8ha (4½ acres), it has an intimate scale.

Prinz-Georgs-Garten leads into Herrengarten, which once held Darmstadt's botanic garden and still has a fine collection of trees. Friedrich Ludwig von Sckell had a hand in its design. There is a magnificent memorial to Prince Emil which lists all the battles he fought in the Napoleonic years. He is dressed as an ancient Viking with a helmet, sword, shield – and nothing else.

open: All year, daily, dawn to dusk

Further information from:
Botanischer Garten und
Arboretum Rombergpark,
Am Rombergpark 49b,
44225-Dortmund
Tel: 0231 5024164

Nearby sights of interest:
The Brauerei-Museum.

Dortmund: Rombergpark

Location: 2km (1¼ miles) S of the city centre

Rombergpark is now a large wooded public park, but it started as an English-style landscape garden early in the 19th century. A fine private collection of trees and shrubs was added before it was acquired by the city authorities in 1927. There is a large lake in the middle, surrounded by handsome tall trees. In fact, many fine trees appear throughout the garden, including magnolias, *Araucaria araucana*, and large *Catalpa bignonioides*. It is best seen in late spring when the azaleas and rhododendrons are in bloom, but it makes a pleasant walk in winter because so much of the underplanting is of evergreen shrubs. Native plants are encouraged to co-exist with planted exotics, and laurels, kalmia and pieris are grown alongside yews and rhododendrons.

The botanic garden is within the park and was founded in 1930. Among its features are geographical plantings, a clematis garden, a heath garden, a conifer collection, and a pretty physic garden, where medicinal plants are displayed in systematic beds.

Dortmund: Westfalenpark

Location: In the town centre

This is one of the most rewarding modern gardens in Germany: no less than 70ha (173 acres) of horticultural display. It was developed after World War II as the West German National Rosarium (Sangerhausen (see p.51) having been lost to the DDR) and contains a collection of over 3,000 different roses, but used in so many ways that the number of rose bushes is closer to 50,000. All are accommodated within a fluid contemporary design which has been entirely changed at least twice since the war. It incorporates some 35 rose gardens each with a different theme, starting with a Romantic Garden, a Jugendstil Garden, and a Medieval Garden, and ending with a beautiful modern rose garden at the eastern end of the park.

Westfalenpark relies for its effect partly upon the spacious design, but also upon the skilful grading of colours and shades, and the lush underplanting. It is a model for the intelligent layout of public gardens. And, although undoubtedly best in early summer, it is much more than just a rose garden. There are steppe gardens, a delphinium garden, fine trees, a phlox garden, collections of climbing plants, a daylily garden, model gardens, large displays of rhododendrons and azaleas, an iris garden, a herb garden, a lake with waterlilies and bog plants, a wild garden, and magnificent displays of bedding. Keen gardeners could spend a week here and never be bored.

open: All year, daily, dawn to dusk

Further information from:
Westfalenpark, 44139-Dortmund
Tel: 06151 26277

Nearby sights of interest:
The television tower (actually inside Westfalenpark) gives magnificent views of industrial Dortmund and the rolling Sauerland.

Westfalenpark is famous for its mixed plantings of roses and herbaceous plants.

open: All year, Mon to Fri,
8am–4pm (closes 2.30pm Fri);
Sat, Sun and Public Holidays,
9am–6pm, Apr to Sep

Further information from:
Botanischer Garten der
Heinrich-Heine-Universität,
40225-Düsseldorf
Tel: 0231 5024164

Nearby sights of interest:
Schloss Benrath, some 4km
(2½ miles) further south.

Düsseldorf: Botanic Garden

Location: In the new university, S of the city

This highly instructive garden was built between 1974 and 1979 on a 7ha (17 acre) green-field site in the new university campus. The systematic collections, some 1,300 taxa representing 220 families, are at its core and offer a good overview of the plant kingdom. The garden's bold and fluid design shows off the plants well. Within it are areas constructed as moraines, screes and volcanic tufa beds, collections of plants from such parts of the world as Japan, North America and the Caucasus, and several interesting horticultural collections. Among the ecological collections are areas devoted to the flora of heathlands, alpine moorlands, coastal sand-dunes and inland sand communities.

The whole garden is dominated by the geodesic dome which houses its principal collection of tender plants. The 3ha (7½ acre) wildflower meadow which surrounds it, best in late spring and early summer, is the perfect foil. This futuristic structure is built of steel and aluminium, and fitted with flexiglass. It covers an area of 1,000 sq m (10,760 sq ft) and is 18m (59ft) high but, because of its design, seems much larger. The house is full of plants from Mediterranean climates. This means that European shrubs like *Erica arborea* rub along with proteas from the Cape, ceanothus from California, callistemons, and xanthorrhoeas from Western Australia. *Echium wildpretti* and other echium species from the Canary Islands are striking in spring.

The geodesic glasshouse dominates the garden.

Düsseldorf: Nordpark

Location: Entrances from Rotterdammerstrasse and Kaiserswertherstrasse

The public parks of Düsseldorf are famous throughout Germany for their public amenities and the high standards of their displays. Nordpark is among the best: 24ha (59 acres) of civic excellence near the International Trade Fair on the sandy banks of the River Rhine. The park was begun in 1937 and laid out in a modern geometrical style with broad walks through grassy lawns and strongly designed floral features. The magnificent formal garden (the Wasserachse) is based upon Baroque precedents but uses contemporary shapes. On the terrace at the end, a vast fountain leads on to a circular formal garden where bedding plants show off a metal mobile that moves in the wind. A formal lily pool is enclosed by a single stone pergola on which wisteria and other climbing plants bloom. Nearby are herbaceous beds, a begonia garden, and swathes of roses planted by the thousands.

But Nordpark has much else besides: magnificent azaleas and rhododendrons, steppe garden plantings, and a good collection of young conifers. And, most remarkable of all, there is a Japanese garden where large pine trees – 10m (33ft) tall – are pruned in the bonsai fashion, with their branches drawn down so that they develop and grow horizontally.

open: All year, daily, dawn to dusk

Further information from:
Nordpark, 40210-Düsseldorf

Nearby sights of interest:
There are two important art galleries in Düsseldorf: the Kunstsammlung Nordrhein-Westfalen and the Kunstmuseum.

The Japanese garden is cared for by local bonsai experts.

Düsseldorf: Schloss Benrath

Location: 10km (6 miles) S of the city centre

Schloss Benrath was built for the Elector Carl Theodor of the Palatinate in 1755 by Nicolas de Pigage. The palace is small, pink and pretty: very Rococo. It sits above a large formal lake, partly enclosed by the two free-standing wings of the palace. The garden was laid out at the same time, but in the 19th century it was landscaped by Peter Joseph Lenné. Since then most of the park's 63ha (156 acres) have been restored to their original Baroque shapes.

Lengthy lime avenues radiate out from the palace, and the main historic garden lies to the south, where a long straight canal stretches away into the woodland. Most of the flowers in the parterre are known to have been available in the 18th century. To the west of the palace, the Elector's private gardens has been restored as a modern public garden, gaily planted with bedding plants and hedged around with rhododendrons and azaleas.

open: All year, daily, dawn to dusk
open: All year, Tue to Sun, 10am–6pm (closes 4pm in winter)

Further information from:
Schloss Benrath, 40597-Düsseldorf
Tel: 0211 3112402

Nearby sights of interest:
Try to visit the palace itself: it forms a perfect unity with the grounds.

Essen: Grugapark

Location: Near Messe (Trade Fair Halls)

open: All year, daily, 9am to dusk

Further information from:
Grugapark und Botanischer Garten, 45133-Essen
Tel: 0201 888507

Nearby sights of interest:
The old Münster in the Burgplatz is one of Essen's historic sights.

This is one of the best civic parks in Germany. It was founded in 1927, redesigned for the Bundesgartenschau in 1965 and now extends to some 70ha (173 acres). At the entrance from the Messegelände the first sight is of a fountain showering five powerful jets of water in parallel arcs, the first of many special features. The whole garden is a *tour de force* of good design and planting, well worth a visit at any time of the year.

Among the highlights are two lakes, good sculptures, a heather garden, a modern rose garden, a state-of-the-art Japanese garden, a model kitchen garden, an ecological garden, a herb garden, a cottage garden, a Mediterranean garden, drifts of candelabra primulas, and an amphitheatre of dahlias. The rock gardens are extensive and include an alpine garden with a mountain stream and waterfall. Better still are the steppe gardens and herbaceous plantings in the natural style used so much in Germany (see p.102). The beautiful dense rhododendron wood is spectacular in late spring. Grugapark also incorporates the botanic garden, which has a fine collection of interesting trees.

Rich herbaceous plantings in the modern style are among Grugapark's many attractions.

Essen: Villa Hügel

Location: Three entrances: easiest from Frieherr-von-Stein-Strasse which follows the N bank of the Rühr

There are three main entrances to this great bastion of German manufacturing power, but it is probably best approached from the south, climbing slowly and reverentially up a grand avenue of plane trees. The garden was laid out in the 1860s and 1870s by Alfried Krupp himself. Impatient for results, and to enjoy the privacy of a woodland garden as soon as possible, he bought semi-mature trees – individual specimens of beech, fir, lime, oak, pine, and plane, each about 50 years old – and brought them here from the surrounding countryside. Exotics were introduced in the 1890s and 1900s by his son and daughter-in-law.

The grandeur of the planting, with beech woodlands and rhododendrons, is awesome. The villa itself is vast, a jumble of architectural styles, but built on a hill top with fine views. The lawns behind the house are the former site of grand Italianate gardens fringed by pergolas and pavilions. These were all swept away when the garden was simplified in the 1950s, though the vases around the house are still richly filled with bedding plants in summer and autumn. Villa Hügel is best in late spring when the rhododendrons are in flower and the horse chestnuts bloom. But it is a place to wander at any time of the year and muse on the might of Germany's greatest industrial family.

open: All year, Tue to Sun, 10am–6pm
open: As above

Further information from:
Villa Hügel, 45127-Essen
Tel: 0201 422 559

Nearby sights of interest:
Museum Folkwang has a good collection of 19th- and 20th-century paintings.

Friedrich Krupp built the "Wendy" house for his daughters.

Frankfurt: Palmengarten

Location: In central Frankfurt: entrances in Siesmayerstrasse and Palmengartenstrasse

Palmengarten is one of the best botanic gardens in Europe: it mixes science with amenity, and botany with horticulture. The scale and excellence of its collections are remarkable, as is the skill with which plants of botanical interest are displayed for the pleasure of visitors. And it is well laid out, with good restaurants, recreation areas and information centres throughout.

The garden was laid out in 1868 and now extends to 20ha (49½ acres). The original palm house is one of the largest in Europe and houses ornamental plants and tree ferns as well as subtropical palms, one of which dates back to the garden's beginnings. The Tropicarium is a vast sequence of glasshouses, divided and planted according to habitat, so that collections can be seen from semi-deserts, savannahs, mangrove swamps, and monsoon regions. Another glasshouse has bromeliads and

open: All year, daily, 9am–6pm (closes 5pm Mar and Oct, 4pm from Nov to Feb)

Further information from:
Palmengarten der Stadt Frankfurt, Siesmayerstr. 61, 60323-Frankfurt-am-Main
Tel: 069 21233939

Nearby sights of interest:
The Cathedral; Goethe's house; the Carmelite cloister and the Historisches Museum.

carnivorous plants: elsewhere are subalpine, subantarctic, and alpine houses. Tender plants are put out in summer, including impressive displays of cacti, fuchsias, palms, and bedding.

The grounds are opulently planted throughout. A formal rose garden with a pergola along one side is bright with modern roses and nearby are collections of old varieties, shrub roses, and scented roses. The Steppe meadows are planted with perennial plants from Europe, Asia and North America, which thrive on well drained soil: maintenance consists of two mowings a year. The rock garden – built 100 years ago but reworked in the 1980s – has mountain plants from all over the world and special areas of gravel, moraine, peat, acid soil, tufa, and rock boulders to suit a whole range of tastes. The Rhododendron garden was planted as recently as 1989 and makes a magnificent display, mainly from *Rhododendron yakushimanum* hybrids.

open: 15 May to 30 Sep, daily, 10am–6pm

Further information from:
Rosengarten Jensen, Am Schlosspark 2b, 24960-Glücksburg
Tel: 04631 60100

Nearby sights of interest:
Glücksburg castle is impressive and full of history.

Glücksburg: Jensen Rose Garden

Location: In the town centre

Ingwer Jensen's show garden is an excellent example of a nurseryman's display garden. It was beautifully designed in 1991 by the late Gunther Schultz, a renowned garden-architect from Hamburg. The central walk leads past an arcade of climbing roses trained on hoops to a semicircle of 'Bonica' roses grown as standards. On one side are model gardens, which make very good use of roses in mixed plantings. On the other side of the central walk are banks of shrub roses in island beds, mainly modern polyanthas interwoven with clematis. A substantial section is devoted to English roses. It is edged with such plants as lavender, which are hardy only in this mild corner of Germany.

Ingwer Jensen's show garden
uses roses as elements of design.

Göttingen: Old and New Botanic Gardens

Location: The old garden is just NE of the old city centre: the new garden is just off An der Luttertal (the road E to the Harz)

open: All year, daily, dawn to dusk

Further information from:
Neuer Botanischer Garten and Altes Botanischer Garten, Untere Karspüle 2, 37073-Göttingen
Tel: 0551 393492

Nearby sights of interest:
The Gänseliesel in the Marktplatz, the statue of "the most kissed girl in the world", whom students embrace when they have passed their final exams.

The old botanic garden was laid out in 1736 in the city's medieval defensive ditch and extends to some 4ha (10 acres). The sunny rock garden is designed mainly geographically, with areas for the plants of Japanese mountains, the southern Alps, the Carpathians and northern Europe. On the shady side of the garden is a collection of ferns and herbaceous plants, including *Darmera peltata*, *Rodgersia podophylla*, and several polygonums. Among the large established trees are *Acer campestre*, *Sorbus torminalis*, and two *Taxodium distichum* by the small lake.

Tunnels lead under the old ramparts to the many glasshouses, which include: a cactus house, a "Victoriahaus" for tropical water plants and epiphytes, a fern house, an overwintering house, a house for Araceae, and a cycad and palm house.

The New Botanic Garden is laid out on a green-field site north-east of the town centre: only nine of its 36 hectares (22 of its 89 acres) have so far been developed. The site is not a pretty one, but for botanical and horticultural interest it is hard to beat. The systematic beds are extensive and include sections for annuals, shrubs, herbaceous perennials, and alpines. The rock garden has many different ecologies: the collection of alpine plants is one of the best in Germany. The arboretum is a model for the intelligent exposition of exotic trees and shrubs.

Traditional systematic beds in Göttingen's Botanic Garden.

Hamburg: Botanic Garden

Location: In Klein Flottbek, W of the city centre

open: All year, daily, 9am–8pm
(closes 4pm in winter)

Further information from:
Botanischer Garten, Hesten 10,
22609-Hamburg
Tel: 040 82282470

Nearby sights of interest:
The boat museum at Ovelgönne,
and discover more about the
maritime history of Hamburg at
the Altonaer Museum.

Hamburg's new botanic garden moved here in 1970 and first
opened to the public in 1979. It replaced the 19th-century Altes
Botanisches Garten in the middle of the city and is attached to
the botany faculty of the University of Hamburg. It has a highly
original modern design that is best appreciated from the circular
concrete islands in the lake – each is connected to the mainland
by wooden pontoons. In fact these are the starting point for a
spacious layout of systematic beds, all devised as a family tree.
Each bed represents a botanical order or section and is planted as
an island in the grass. A narrow path links it to its neighbours and
illustrates the development of botanical divisions, classes, orders,
and families. It is one of those clever designs that is easier to
appreciate once a plan has been seen on paper. Around the
outside of these systematic beds is a "geographic" collection of
plants, laid out to copy their natural distribution according to the
pre-Linnaean system. So there are sections for China and Japan,
for example, all displayed in a stylized map of the globe.

Certain plants have distinct areas dedicated to them: there
are excellent collections of conifers and rhododendrons, a large
rock garden, and beds devoted to daylilies, modern roses, and
irises. Especially popular – for the garden is intended to delight
its visitors – are a Japanese stone garden and a cottage garden
in front of a little thatched summerhouse.

Vertically-thrusting, colourful
mixed plantings are set off
by the mounted brass globe.

Hamburg: Planten un Blomen

Location: In the city centre

Hamburg has a wonderful series of public parks along the edge of the old city fortifications. The gardens that connect the TV tower in the north of the city to the river in the south are one continuous walk, 2.5km (1½ miles) long. Planten un Blomen is one of the best modern civic gardens in Germany, at its peak in early summer when the rhododendrons give way to the roses, but rewarding to visit whatever the season. It now incorporates the old botanic garden. It is renowned for its Japanese garden, which is the largest in Europe. The focal point is a thatched tea-house in the middle of a lake. Nearby is a spectacular rose garden, where blocks of modern roses are grown in beds, augmented by tubular arches trained with roses, and clematis.

Throughout the garden, large areas are given to seasonal bedding, steppe plantings and ground-cover plants: there are vast patches of astilbes, bergenias, daylilies, geraniums, hostas, and polygonatums. There are also some fine trees, especially on the leafy sides of the steep valley which run down to the lake in the old botanic garden. Well positioned modern sculptures decorate the garden. The greenhouses were built for the International Garden Show in 1963: they include a tropical house, cycad house, subtropical house, fern house, and succulent house.

open: All year, daily, dawn to dusk

Further information from:
Planten und Blomen,
20095-Hamburg
Tel: 0551 397822

Nearby sights of interest:
See the busy Aussenalster and allow lots of time for the magnificent Kunsthalle.

The Japanese garden was designed in 1991 by Professor Yoshikumi Araki.

121

Hanau: Wilhelmsbad

Location: 3km (1¾ miles) NW of Hanau

open: All year, daily, dawn to dusk

Further information from:
Wilhelmsbad, 63454-Hanau
Tel: 040 82282470

Nearby sights of interest:
Schloss Philippsruhe, 2km (1¼ miles) south, is a handsome Baroque palace.

Wilhelmsbad is one of the earliest English landscape parks in Germany. It was laid out from 1777 onwards by Hereditary Prince Wilhelm of Hessen-Kassel, who lived at nearby Hanau while he was crown prince. He built it as a spa, to bring money and prestige to his principality, and landscaped the 38ha (94 acre) park with artistic ruins which are the forerunners of Löwenburg at Kassel (see p.130). First he excavated a lake, then built a Gothic castle on an island in the middle: the ruined exterior concealed comfortable living quarters for the prince. Nearby is a fortified gatehouse, also built as a ruin to incorporate the kitchens, and a pyramid on a second island (somewhat incongruous, but built as a melancholy memorial). Spoil from the lake was used to make a tall mound. A winding path snakes up its sides (note the pretty, white Chinese-style railings) and gives a good view of the whole landscape, particularly in winter when the prospect is not obscured by trees in leaf. Excavations were also used to add hummocks to the park, many of which are planted with beech. An ancient carousel was constructed with horses and carriages under a domed cupola in 1779: it was originally made to revolve by manpower, but later by horses. Nearby are the Devil's Bridge and an artificial gorge that leads out into a wilderness.

When Prince Wilhelm moved to Kassel in 1785, Wilhelmsbad fell out of fashion, so it represents a well preserved example of landscaping for an 18th-century German spa.

Prince Wilhelm's pyramid on an island in the artificial lake.

Hanover: Botanic Garden

Location: Immediately N of Herrenhausen

Hanover's botanic garden is known as the Berggarten. Originally a kitchen garden for the royal household, it has had a purely botanical function since about 1750. It was landscaped in the 19th century and remade after extensive bomb damage in World War II. Modern plantings have been beautifully integrated into the spacious design: it is one of the most accessible and "horticultural" gardens in Germany.

Near the entrance, at the south-east corner, are several pretty display gardens: an iris garden; a rock garden; and a pergola garden designed by Karl Förster. Along the western boundary, a double line of lime trees leads up to the mausoleum of the Kings of Hanover. Herbaceous plants are grown here in great masses: it is one of the best collections in Germany. Nearby is *Fagus sylvatica* 'Suenteliensis', a totally prostrate form of common beech, which droops over an iron arcade and covers a large area.

Most of the garden's trees were destroyed in the war, but the oldest cucumber tree *(Magnolia acuminata)*, in Germany survived, as did a 150-year-old *Taxodium distichum*, and a magnificent specimen of *Fagus sylvatica* 'Albovariegata'. But the high point is the design of the Paradiesgarten – a glade of heathers edged with magnolias and Kurume azaleas at the end of a long walk up from the gate: it is a work of genius. The glasshouses include a major collection of cacti and succulents. And it was here that African violets *(Saintpaulia ionantha)* first bloomed in Europe.

open: All year, daily, 8am–8pm (closes 4.30pm in winter)

Further information from:
Berggarten, Herrenhäuser Str. 4, 30149-Hanover
Tel: 0511 1687576

Nearby sights of interest:
Other good gardens in the Herrenhausen complex include the Georgengarten and the Guelph Garden.

The Paradiesgarten in Hanover's Botanic Garden (the Berggarten) is a work of genius.

Hanover: Herrenhausen

Location: NW of the city centre, well signposted

open: All year, daily,
8am–8pm (closes 4pm in winter)

Further information from:
Grosser Garten, Herrenhausen,
30159-Hanover
Tel: Hanover tourist office
0511 301422

Nearby sights of interest:
The Kestermuseum (decorative
arts) and the Niedersächsisches
Landesmuseum (fine arts,
archaeology and natural history).

Herrenhausen was the summer residence of the Dukes and Electors of Hanover. The garden was begun in 1665 by Duke Johann Friedrich. The oldest structure here is the Great Cascade, near the entrance, which dates from 1676 and is embellished with shells, stalactites, and sculptures – a stylistic link to the gardens of the Italian Renaissance. It was the Duke's daughter-in-law the Electress Sophia (mother of George I of England) who reorganised the original design; she added so many decorative details that it is now is largely her monument. Indeed, she described the gardens at Herrenhausen as her life's work.

Herrenhausen owes its preservation to Sophia's English connection.

Strange gilded statues line
the wings of the open-air
hedge theatre.

George I's mother, the Electress
Sophia, described the garden
as her life's work.

The Great Fountain is capable of reaching 82m (269ft) high.

Stately fountains fill the quarters of the New Garden.

When George I inherited the English throne, he and his descendants moved to London: Herrenhausen therefore escaped the ravages of the landscape movement. The sad thing is that the palace, which was the centrepiece of the gardens, was destroyed in the last war and, unlike the majority of historic buildings in Germany, has never been rebuilt. The garden was thoroughly over-restored in the 1930s, when all manner of charming but quite unhistorical additions were made. They add so much to the character of the garden that it is now impossible to imagine it without them.

The gardens at Herrenhausen are very big. Even though their design and layout are formal and simple, it takes a long time – and much walking – to become acquainted with all their ornaments, details, and secrets. The first thing you see is the Grand Parterre, which is approximately 200 sq m (2,152 sq ft): its beds have highly elaborate *broderies* and are richly planted with seasonal bedding. The ground plan is tricked out with elaborate vases and sculptures of gods, seasons, virtues and continents. There are 32 of them, all painted bright white to make them stand out more brilliantly against the parterres. The large circular Bell Fountain has 166 jets in the centre and is especially beautiful when floodlit at night. It dates from 1936: the original design had a mere 25 jets.

In 1692 the Electress Sophia extended the garden by taking in another 25ha (62 acres), roughly square, which effectively doubled its size. The extension is still called the New Garden.

Endymion is one of the 32 white-painted statues in the Grand Parterre.

Between it and the Grand Parterre are four square ponds known as the Swan Lakes. Though later modified, they date back to 1679 and were originally used for keeping fish and waterfowl. They back onto eight enclosed gardens, hidden behind tall hedges, designed in 1936 to show off different aspects of garden history. These popular but unhistorical pastiches are called: the Renaissance Garden, Baroque Garden, North German Flower Garden, Rococo Garden, Island Garden, Spring-water Garden, Lawn Garden, and North German Rose Garden. Just beyond them is a glamorous 19th-century marble statue of the Electress Sophia at exactly the spot where she died of a sudden heart attack on 8 June 1714 – she missed being Queen of England by only a few days.

The New Garden was laid out between 1699 and 1709. It is divided into squares and triangles by formal *bosquets* and diagonal avenues. Each of its four quarters has an octagonal pool with a fountain at its middle. One very impressive feature of the New Garden is the way that its elements are linked to each other, fountain to fountain, over long distances: it reinforces the sense of scale. At its furthest end are two handsome identical pavilions, which date from 1706 but were rebuilt in their present form in the 1750s. At the centre of the whole garden is the Great Fountain, capable of blowing a single jet of water high into the air at speeds of up to 140kph (87mph).

The open air theatre is lined with curious statues of gilded lead.

However, it is the Grand Parterre which is the centre of the garden. Off to one side is the Fig Garden where apricots and peaches are cultivated in forcing frames. This is matched on the other side by a parterre where orange trees in pots are put outside the old orangery building for the summer months. It dates from 1965. Nearby is the Hedge Theatre, laid out between 1689 and 1692 and still used for summer performances. Its narrow, deep stage has hornbeam hedges with numerous exits and entrances in the wings and is lined with curious Dutch figures of gilded lead. The maze, on the other side of the Grand Parterre, was added in 1937 and is therefore not original. The same is true of the adjacent Viewing Terrace. The wooden colonnaded temples were also 1937 additions which were built to a Dutch design.

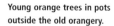

Young orange trees in pots outside the old orangery.

Herrenhausen's garden provokes more admiration than affection. It has none of the humour of the Baroque gardens of southern Germany and the Rhineland, nor does it display the invention of the gardens at Kassel and Potsdam. Throughout the garden the urge to magnificence is tempered by a cold northern restraint.

open: Apr to Sep, daily,
10am–7pm

Further information from:
Insel Siebenbergen, 34121-Kassel
Tel: 0561 1687576

Nearby sights of interest:
Karlsaue itself is essential visiting
for lovers of historic gardens.

26 *Kassel: Insel Siebenbergen*

Location: At the SW end of Karlsauerpark

Siebenbergen is a moated island at the furthest tip of Karlsaue (see opposite) and has been managed quite distinctly for many years. It is in effect a horticultural showpiece, arguably the most "English" garden in Germany, where plants of every kind are grown together for artistic effect. The planting is nothing less than luxuriant and the standard of maintenance incomparable.

The garden is reached over an elegant iron footbridge. It began as an arboretum with fine conifers: a vast specimen of the oriental spruce *Picea orientalis* has rooted out from the base and produced three satellite trees. Among the many interesting deciduous trees are *Fagus sylvatica* 'Asplenifolia', *Quercus robur* 'Concordia', and *Pawlonia tomentosa*. Evergreen shrubs are the backbone of the structural planting. But there are also deciduous shrubs, such as azaleas and hydrangeas, as well as a magnificent display of fuchsias. The rich herbaceous plantings include hostas, primulas, and pulmonarias, among scores of plants in sweeps and drifts. They are supplemented by spectacular summer bedding.

The island rises steeply to its centre. A rock garden lines the sides of the path to the top of the hill, which is flat and filled with a huge circular bed brightly planted with a complex array of bedding plants. Paths run off to secluded bays and conspicuous vantage points. There are wonderful views over the Karlsaue towards the temple on Schwaneninsel and the Orangeriepalais in the distance. It is impossible to praise this garden too much.

Insel Siebenbergen is a horticultural paradise, and meticulously maintained.

Kassel: Karlsaue

Location: W of the city centre

The Baroque orangery palace at the centre of Karlsaue was built between 1701 and 1711 by Landgraf Karl, who also laid out a vast and complex formal garden. The garden's shape is roughly rhomboidal, with the palace at one end and the Siebenbergen island (see opposite) at the other. It is about 2km (1¼ miles) long and 1km (½ mile) wide at its broadest point. The view from the palace is a perfect *patte d'oie*. Two long canals bordered by avenues of German oaks *(Quercus robur)* lead off to the sides. The central ride has double avenues and runs through woodland towards distant Siebenbergen. The view ends in a temple perched on an island (Schwaneninsel) in a formal Baroque lake.

Around the sides of the immense lawn below the orangery palace are tubs of orange trees, oleanders, and pomegranates, while the terraces are lined with palms, agapanthus and bay trees in white Versailles tubs. The prospect is one of the grandest in all Germany. At the end of the formal lawn lies a semicircle of white-painted sandstone statues which stand against a bosky background of young oaks.

Elector Wilhelm I changed the Baroque garden into a land-scaped park in the 1790s. It was altered again between 1820 and 1850 when many exotic plantings were added, and again in the 20th century to accommodate two Bundesgartenschauen. Now it resembles stately parkland planted with handsome individual trees. And the Baroque ground plan is still stupendous.

open: All year, daily, dawn to dusk

Further information from:
Karlsaue, 34117-Kassel
Tel: Kassel tourist office
0561 34054

Nearby sights of interest:
The "Orangeriepalais" houses a Museum of Astronomy, open all year, Tue to Sun 10am–5pm.

The temple on Schwaneninsel is the focal point at Karlsaue and the garden of Insel Siebenbergen.

28 # Kassel: Wilhelmshöhe

Location: 4km (2½ miles) W of the city centre

open: All year, daily, dawn to dusk

open: All year, Tue to Sun, 10am–4pm (closes 3pm Nov to Feb)

Further information from:
Wilhelmshöhe, 34131-Kassel
Tel: 0561 18809

Nearby sights of interest:
The state art gallery in the palace is a must: eleven Rembrandts among many other 17th-century Dutch and Flemish paintings.

The waterfall which runs down from Hercules' pyramid is only the start of the majestic landcape.

Wilhelmshöhe is the most important historic garden in Hesse and one of the most ambitious Baroque gardens in Germany. The park extends to nearly 1000ha (2,471 acres) and there is a difference in altitude of 288m (945ft) between the highest and lowest points. There are car parks at the top and the bottom, but the distances are considerable and a visit involves much walking, so allow plenty of time.

Landgraf Karl of Kassel employed Gianfrancesco Guerniero to lay out the formal garden between 1699 and 1700. The Landgraf was much influenced by the gardens he had seen in while travelling in Italy. The centrepoint of the design is the steep mountain behind the palace which is crowned by a colossal statue of Hercules (now the symbol of the city of Kassel) on an Olympian octagonal pedestal. The mountainside is riven with dramatic cascades, pools, and grottoes set amid rocky outcrops and sublime spruces.

Landgraf Friedrich II developed the park and planted many trees from 1760 to 1785. Then Wilhelm IX (the Elector Wilhelm I) landscaped the mountainside in the 1790s, added a pretty Ionic temple to Apollo close to the palace and the Devil's Bridge

halfway up near a grotto named after Pluto. Wilhelm also built a ruined Roman aqueduct, which delivers an elemental force of water, and he commissioned H J Jussow to build the mock-medieval neo-Gothic ruined castle called the Schloss Löwenburg, which was constructed between 1794 and 1798. All are substantial, dramatic, and impressive buildings. There were further developments in the 19th century: the pretty conservatory, for example, was added in 1822.

In modern times, a large and important collection of old species and other shrub roses has been planted around the big lake at the bottom. Nor is horticulture absent: the woods around Wilhelmshöhe are particularly enjoyable when the rhododendrons are in full bloom in late spring. But it is the sight of the water pouring down the majestic mountainside which is the abiding memory of Wilhelmshöhe for most visitors.

Kassel: Schloss Wilhelmstal

Location: 9km (5½ miles) N of Wilhelmshöhe

Wilhelmstal was the summer residence of Landgrave Wilhelm VIII of Hessen-Kassel and, to this day, the drive up from Wilhelmshöhe still passes through beautiful valleys and woods. The pretty Rococo palace at Wilhelmstal was matched in the 1750s by a complex and extensive Rococo garden whose axes all fanned out from the principal rooms. Both the palace and its garden are best visited in the afternoon when the sun lights up the landscape from behind.

The most famous feature was built in 1756 and restored in the 1960s: a long canal leading up to an elegant pavilion, decorated with gilded statues and fountains. It is flanked by a double avenue of maples. Wilhelm IX (the Elector William I) remodelled the garden in the landscape style, and so it remains today.

At the back of the palace, beyond some modern herbaceous plantings, is a lake which leads the eye beyond, over mounds of grass, along a lengthy avenue and away into the distance. A neo-Gothic watchtower crowns the hilltop. It is surrounded by idyllic classical English landscaping: one can only imagine the splendour and extent of the original Baroque layout.

open: All year, Tue to Sun, 10am–5pm (closes 4pm Nov to Feb)
open: As above

Further information from:
Wilhelmsthal, 34379-Calden
Tel: 0567 46898

Nearby sights of interest:
Visit Wilhelmshöhe, the greatest historic garden in Hessen.

The elegant pavilion at the end of the canal is flanked by statues.

Kiel: Botanic Garden

Location: In the new university, NW of the city centre

The wide variety of plants in Kiel's botanic garden is best seen in late spring and early summer, and there is much to interest the keen home gardener. Advantage has been taken of the sandy soil to plant trees that relish the conditions, such as *Sorbus* and cultivars of *Fagus sylvatica*, including some rare ones. Conifers have been nicely planted, with open grassy areas around them.

The entrance leads through a highly colourful open courtyard planted with modern roses and bedding plants, past the excellent systematic beds to a magnificent rock garden. The spacious layout makes it possible to walk on the rocks to look closely at the plants and study them. They are laid out geographically though a certain amount of intercontinental naturalization is tolerated. The garden also has an important collection of South African succulents. Only the distant traffic of the ring road around Kiel detracts from the pleasure of visiting this garden.

open: All year, daily, 9am–6pm (closes 5pm Mar and Oct, 4pm Nov to Feb)

Further information from:
Botanischer Garten der Universität, Olshausenstr. 40, 24118-Kiel
Tel: 0431 8804276

Nearby sights of interest:
There is a charming museum of country life in Schleswig-Holstein called the Freilichtmuseum (at Molfsee).

Krefeld: Botanic Garden

Location: Signposted from Berliner Strasse

open: Apr to Oct, daily,
8am–6pm; Nov to Mar, Mon to Fri,
9am–3pm (closes 12 noon Fri)

Further information from:
Botanischer Garten der Stadt
Krefeld, 47809-Krefeld
Tel: 02151 540519

Nearby sights of interest:
Visit the German textile
museum at Linn.

Begun as a teaching garden in 1913, Krefeld Botanic Garden was enlarged in 1928 to its present size of 4ha (10 acres). It is an attractive and instructive garden, now maintained by the town of Krefeld: its motto "Freude mit Blumen" ("Joy with Flowers"), is tricked out in box hedging beside the main entrance.

The garden has developed a distinct mission – to satisfy the needs of local people and their gardens. Large areas are devoted to plants of horticultural merit that will be of interest and value to people in their own gardens. These include extensive displays of annuals and herbaceous plants, a rose garden, spring bulbs, begonia trials, a display of dahlias, and permanent plantings of such shrubs as tamarisk varieties, which are particularly suited to the sandy soil of Krefeld.

All the designs are modern. The collection of herbaceous plants of garden value is grown in circular systematic beds. The roses are mainly new or recent introductions, and there is a small collection of shrub and species roses. The rock garden incorporates some raised beds and ground-cover plants. Orchids and tender plants are put out for the summer, but the mild climate allows such trees as *Araucaria aracauna* and *Cunninghamia lanceolata* to flourish outside.

Krefeld Botanic Garden has displays of plants that grow well in local gardens.

Lütetsburg: Schlosspark

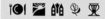

Location: 3km (1¾ miles) E of Norden

The red-brick Wasserburg Lütetsburg is one of the finest historic
buildings in the remote countryside of East Friesland. Its
park was laid out in the anglo-*chinois* style in the 1790s by Carl
Ferdinand Bosse and replaced an earlier Baroque garden. It was
extended to 40ha (99 acres) in 1812 and has been dramatically
improved by new planting since the 1930s.

The entrance is some distance to the side of the castle, and
lined with golden conifers. This narrow approach is modest
compared to the size and magnificence of the garden, a perfect
18th-century landscape enhanced by modern plantings. The park
seems to stretch endlessly into the surrounding woodland of oak
and beech. It is traversed by white sandy paths and sinuous
watercourses that barely move. White *chinois* bridges and white-
painted seats tack the parkland together. Beyond the octagonal
cottage orné are a rustic chapel made of wood and, further still, a
Temple of Friendship: all date from the end of 18th century.
Great banks of rhododendrons and azaleas thrive in the mild
maritime climate and flower spectacularly in spring. There are
laurels, pieris, and zenobias too: hydrangeas and *Aesculus parviflora*
extend the season into autumn. Good trees abound: though none
is named, there is much for the knowledgeable dendrologist.

open: All year, daily,
8am–9pm (closes 5pm Oct to Apr)

Further information from:
Lütetsburg, 26524-Lütetsburg
Tel: 0431 8804276

Nearby sights of interest:
Norden and Aurich are both worth
a visit: nearby Norddeich is the
ferry port for Juist and Norderney,
two of the Friesian islands.

The charming *cottage orné* can
be seen from much of the garden.

Münster: Botanic Garden

Location: In grounds of the Castle

open: All year, daily,
8am–7pm (closes 5pm in winter)

Further information from:
Botanischer Garten,
48143-Münster
Tel: 02151 833810

Nearby sights of interest:
Burg Hülshoff, just north-west of
the city, was the birthplace of the
poet Annette von Droste-Hülshoff.

The alpine garden is neatly
maintained and is also
instructively planted.

Münster Botanic Garden was first laid out in 1804 as a physic garden for the medical faculty of the newly founded university, on the instructions of Friedrich Wilhelm III of Prussia. Its site was once part of the park attached to the palace of the Prince Bishops. The present garden is neatly designed to include a large number of interesting and instructive features within its 4ha (10 acres). At its centre is a well maintained area devoted to systematic beds, incorporating a small exhibition garden of Fleuroselect plants. Nearby is a rock garden, perched above a small lake filled with waterlilies. The shady parts of the garden support a fern garden and a good collection of azaleas. Other areas are devoted to the study of particular ecologies, including birch woods, dry sandy soils, chalky beech woods, alkaline steppe communities, and moorland set around a boggy pond.

Among the many attractive trees in the arboretum are a gnarled multi-trunked Turkish hazel, *Corylus colurna*, and an exceptionally slender form of the Serbian spruce, *Picea omorika*. The arboretum is underplanted with rhododendrons and other ericaceous shrubs. Everything is well labelled and there are helpful boards with detailed descriptions of what each feature of the garden seeks to teach. The glasshouses include a Canary Island house, a "Victoriahaus", a succulent house, a bromeliad house, a Cape house, and a palm-cum-fern house.

Nordkirchen: Schlossgarten

Location: Signposted in the village

Nordkirchen is a red-brick Wasserburg, surrounded by a double moat and set in the misty marshes of the Münsterland. It was built between 1703 and 1733 for the Prince Bishop of Münster, Friedrich Christian von Plettenberg and was once known as the Westphalian Versailles: it remains the largest Baroque château in present-day Westphalia.

The original Dutch and French gardens have long since disappeared. The present formal garden, on the north side of the castle, is a reconstruction of a neo-Baroque layout made between 1906 and 1914 for the then Duke of Arenberg by Achille Duchêne, the celebrated French designer who was also responsible for the formal garden at Blenheim Palace, near Oxford. It is laid out between the two moats, and remains a very grand formal garden. The elaborate central parterre is filled with coloured gravel: the simpler outer ones have lawns with ribbons of seasonal bedding around their outsides. The parterres are of box, with cones of yew and privet, grown as standards. The decoration is with urns, and statues of hounds and hogs: the Duke was keen on hunting. There are also figures of nymphs, goddesses, and fauns, and busts of such worthies as Socrates and Homer, set on plinths.

The surrounding park is thickly wooded with avenues of dark purple beeches. The garden remains a handsome example of the German aptitude for the restoration of historic gardens, even though many purists would prefer to see a reconstruction of the original Baroque designs in place of Duchêne's pastiche.

open: All year, daily, dawn to dusk
open: All year, Sat and Sun, 2–5pm

Further information from:
Schloss Nordkirchen,
59394-Nordkirchen
Tel: 02596 1001

Nearby sights of interest:
The Münsterland Museum at Burg Vischering.

Hunting figures add great character to the parterres.

Oldenburg: Botanic Garden

Location: W of the city centre, near the ring road

Oldenburg's homely botanic garden was established in 1882 and extends to 3.7ha (9 acres). As well as the usual systematic beds it has geographical and habitat borders, and a good collection of grasses. Areas are set aside for native plants, especially those which grow on the sandy soil of north-west Germany and have adapted to survive with very little nutrient. The garden profits from the mild climate and many of the plants, including *Rhododendron x loderi*, are not hardy in most of Germany. There are large specimens of *Metasequoia glyptostroboides* and *Cunninghamia lanceolata*, and an elegant grove of *Picea breweriana* with graceful, pendulous branches. In many ways it is most reminiscent of an English park.

open: All year, daily, 8am–5pm (stays open later in summer)

Further information from:
Botanischer Garten der Universität Oldenburg, Philosophenweg 41,
26121-Oldenburg
Tel: 0441 71636

Nearby sights of interest:
The great nurseries of Rastede are about 6km (3¾ miles) to the north.

Oldenburg: Schlossgarten

Location: In the city centre

open: All year, daily, dawn to dusk

Further information from:
Schlossgarten, 26122-Oldenburg
Tel: Oldenburg tourist office
0441 15744

Nearby sights of interest:
The Stadtmuseum in the old Grand-Ducal Schloss has a magnificent collection of paintings by J H W Tischbein.

The Schlossgarten at Oldenburg extends to 16.5ha (41 acres) and was laid out between 1806 and 1817 in the landscape style by Carl Ferdinand Bosse. It is a sequence of long, flowing, spacious glades. The parkland trees have grown to a considerable height and huge clumps of rhododendron, mainly *Rhododendron ponticum*, have been planted round a large lake. The open, grassed areas are perfectly in scale with the tall trees and the vast hummocks of rhododendrons at their sides. The woodland makes for delightful walking in late spring and early summer when they are in full bloom. The drifts of the yellow azalea, *R. lutea*, and the late-flowering hardy hybrid evergreens are especially attractive. Among the many good specimen trees is a clump of four very large tulip trees, *Liriodendron tulipifera*.

Sögel: Schloss Clemenswerth

Location: 1km (½ mile) E of Sögel

open: All year, daily, dawn to dusk
open: Apr to Oct, Tue to Sun, 10am–12.30pm and 2–6pm

Further information from:
Schloss Clemenswerth,
49751-Sögel
Tel: 0595 21077

Nearby sights of interest:
One of the eight pavilions contains the Emsland Museum.

The flower garden is enclosed by ancient yew hedges.

The Baroque park surrounding Schloss Clemenswerth was made by Johann Conrad Schlaun for the Elector Clemens August of Cologne between 1737 and 1749. Eight straight avenues of oak and lime radiate out into the woods like points and half-points of the compass. Schlaun's original drawings show that the woodland on either side of these avenues was enclosed by high clipped hedges and around the outside of the 64ha (158 acres) was an elaborate system of ornamental pools and canals.

Schloss Clemenswerth itself sits at the centre of the star, the focus of the entire design. It is a small hunting lodge, surrounded by eight pavilions that are identical on the outside though used for different purposes: one, for example, is an exquisite Rococo chapel. Behind that chapel is a garden enclosed within ancient overgrown crenellated yew hedges. This chunky topiary dates back to the original garden 250 years ago and is one of the few places in Germany where one can see the billowing bulk of centuries-old clipped yew. The garden which it encircles has four central paths with an astrolabe in the middle and box-edged herbaceous borders. The planting is appropriately spare: simple, open, and spacious.

Uetersen: Rose Garden

Location: In the town centre

open: All year, daily, dawn to dusk

Further information from:
Rosarium Uetersen,
25436-Uetersen

Nearby sights of interest:
West of Uetersen, towards the coast, is a land of dykes, canals, bleak landscapes rich in bird-life.

Rosarium Uetersen was founded in 1929 and opened in 1934. It was the brainchild of two important German rose nurseries: Tantau of Uetersen and Kordes of nearby Sparrieshoop. The 7ha (17 acre) park is laid out around two lakes whose banks are planted with old weeping willows. Rhododendrons and fine conifers make an evergreen background to the roses which are, of course, the principal feature of the garden.

Rosarium Uetersen is a fascinating place for anyone who wants to see what is available from rose nurseries and how it looks in a garden. There are more than 30,000 roses representing some 830 different varieties: many are modern German hybrids from Tantau and Kordes. Beds are cut out of the grass and each devoted to one variety: with up to several hundred specimens in a single bed the effect is highly colourful. Along one side, climbing and rambling roses are trained up rough metal tripods. There are also a few old roses and such curiosities as the green rose, *Rosa chinensis* 'Viridiflora'. And of course there is the rose 'Rosarium Uetersen' itself, a deep pink scented variety with a mass of old-fashioned ruffled petals in the centre of the flower: it is one of the best modern climbers.

Bright modern rose cultivars dominate the garden at Uetersen.

🍽️ 📷 🏛️ 🏰

🏵️ **open:** All year, daily, dawn to dusk

🏛️ **open:** All year, Tue to Sun, 10am–4pm

Further information from:
Schlossgarten, 35871-Weilburg
Tel: 05952 527

Nearby sights of interest:
Wander round the town itself and admire its beautiful position.

Cast iron balustrading and urns: a unique feature of Weilburg.

39 *Weilburg: Schlossgarten*

Location: In the town centre

Nothing remains of the Baroque garden laid out by Graf Johann Ernst of Nassau early in the 18th century: most of the present garden at Weilburg was reconstructed in the 1930s. The formal garden by the palace was made in 1936: the fountain and figures are 18th century but were brought here from Büdesheim in 1967. Two very large copper beeches stand guard nearby. Along the edge of the upper garden, which overlooks the valley, is some unusual cast iron balustrading dating from 1706. The beautiful cast iron urns along the top and the handsome balustrading are all tricked out in grey-blue and gold paint. At the end of the upper terrace is an attractive area shaded by pollarded, trained limes. These are a genuine reconstruction: the originals were planted between 1758 and 1759 to connect the upper garden with the lower. From the roof of the old orangery there is a view down to this formal garden with its laurels in tubs, two gilded statues and trained pear trees: the sundial dates from 1694. From here a stately staircase leads down to the lower parterre. The simple grass parterres are edged with flamboyant summer bedding. The old orangery is now a delightful café.

Wuppertal: Botanic Garden

Location: Difficult: buy a street plan

open: All year , daily, 7.30am–7pm (closes 6pm Mar and Oct, 5pm Nov to Feb)

Further information from:
Botanischer Garten, Elisenhöhe 1, 42103-Wuppertal
Tel: 0202 5634207

Nearby sights of interest:
Ride on the Schwebebahn, Wuppertal's overhead monorail railway.

This charming small garden was started by the town fathers of Elberfeld as a school garden and did not become the Wuppertal Botanic Garden until the town of Wuppertal was created in 1929. Its focal point is the pink Elisenturm, a tower which is 21.4m (70ft) high and crowns the highest point of the 2.5ha (6 acre) garden. Some 4,000 taxa are grown here. Among the best trees are a huge trifurcating bird cherry, *Prunus avium*, a tall *Liriodendron tulipiferum*, an old purple beech and some pretty magnolias. The garden is attractive in spring, when naturalized *Cyclamen coum* var. *caucasicum* are succeeded by daffodils and many plants come into flower in the rock garden. Other features include a rhododendron walk, a small steppe garden, and a physic garden. There is a stylish display of tender plants on the terraces in front of the house. Nearby are a succulent house and a warm-water tank where *Victoria amazonica* is grown every year.

Zweibrücken: Europas Rose Garden

Location: Signposted in the town

open: Apr to Oct, daily, 8am–7pm

Further information from:
Europas Rosengarten, 66482-Zweibrücken
Tel: 06332 871123

Even in October, Zweibrücken's Rose Garden is full of colour.

Europas Rose Garden boasts more than 60,000 roses in 2,000 different varieties. All are clearly labelled, which makes this an excellent place to learn about the different types. But this splendid civic park is not just a rose garden: it also offers good displays of annuals, herbaceous plants, irises, and 5ha (12 acres) around a lake, designed as a constantly changing sequence of gardens. Although it was first opened in 1914, and some of the trees date from then, the layout is contemporary, with modern sculptures and such international features as a Canadian totem pole.

Europas Rosengarten is a source of much pride in Zweibrücken, and popular for weddings. A 2.5km (1½ mile) walkway and cycleway links it to the wild rose garden in the garden of the Pleasure Palace of the Polish King Stanislaus Lesczynsky. Here are 1,000 species and shrubs which tell the story of hybridization, a living museum of the ancestors of our modern roses.

Glossary

Art Nouveau (French) Literally "new art", a style of decorative and fine arts originating in the 1890s, associated with sinuous flowing lines and stylized natural forms.

baldachino (Italian) A structure in the form of a canopy, borne on ornate columns.

belvedere (Italian) An ornamental building in some commanding position from which a view may be admired.

bosquet (French) A formal grove, often with a decorative glade in which statues or other ornaments may be disposed.

broderies (French) Ornate parterres with flowing designs which imitate embroidery patterns.

Bundesgartenschau (German) National garden shows which take place in a new location every two years and last for several months. Before World War II these were known as *Reichsgartenschau*.

Chinois (French) A Chinese fashion in the decorative arts that was especially popular in England and Germany in the 18th century.

cottage orné (French) Literally, "ornamental cottage". A small rustic building, often thatched, which is used as a picturesque feature in a landscape garden.

cour d'honneur (French) The main entrance court of a great house.

cupola (Italian) A small structure, usually domed, on the top of a church or ornamental building.

gotico fiorito (Italian) An ornamental style of Gothic decoration which reached the peak of its expression in Venice c1500.

jardin secret (French) Literally, a secret (or hidden) garden.

Jugendstil (German) The German for *Art Nouveau*; the name of an art journal started in 1896.

Landesgartenschau (German) Provincial garden shows which take place in a different location every two years and last for several months.

parterre (French) A formal bedding with low hedges, often of box, disposed in a regular way and often incorporating topiary, urns, or other decorative devices. A *parterre de broderie* is a particular form in which the shapes are arranged in long flowing patterns.

patte d'oie (French) Literally a goose-foot. An arrangement of three alleys or avenues radiating from a central point; especially associated with the gardens of Le Nôtre.

putti (Italian) Ornamental cherubs, especially associated with Baroque architecture, painting, and gardens.

quincunx (Latin) A formal garden of four geometric beds arranged around a fifth central bed.

trompe l'oeil (French) A style of painting in which objects are depicted as three-dimensional; literally "deceive the eye".

Victoriahaus (German) A tropical waterlily glasshouse, whose botanical showpiece is one or both species of Victoria.

Biographies

Anhalt-Dessau, Prince Franz von (1740–1817) German landowner much influenced by enlightened English ideas concerning agriculture and industry. He introduced the neo-Gothic style to Germany, and from 1764 he and his gardeners J G Schoch and J F Eyserbeck created the 150 sq km (58 sq miles) *Gartenreich* along the Elbe, which included Wörlitz, Luisium, and Oranienbaum.

Bosse, Carl Ferdinand German garden designer who worked at the gardens of Lütetsburg, Rastede, and Dyck at the end of the 18th century.

Effner, Karl von Court gardener to the Kings of Bavaria during the middle of the 19th century.

Eyserbeck, Johann August (1762–1801) German garden designer who worked at Oranienbaum, Dresden, Sanssouci, and Charlottenburg. Son of J F Eyserbeck.

Eyserbeck, Johann Friedrich (1734–1818) German garden designer and court gardener at Luisium and at Dessau, where he worked for Prince Franz von Anhalt-Dessau.

Förster, Carl (1874–1970) German nurseryman, plant breeder, designer, and garden writer, especially concerned to integrate natural planting with public landscape design.

Girard, Dominique (d1738) French garden designer who, influenced by working as a young man at Versailles, designed gardens at Clemenswerth, Nymphenburg, and Schleissheim in Germany.

Goethe, Johann Wolfgang von (1749–1832) German polymath, poet, novelist, and dramatist, the founder of modern German literature, and leader of the Romantic *Sturm und Drang* movement.

Lenné, Peter Josef (1789–1866) The leading 19th-century German landscape designer, who worked throughout Germany although he is perhaps best known for his arrangement of the landscape around Potsdam.

Le Nôtre, André (1630–1700) French garden designer and director of building to Louis XIV. He strongly influenced the development of gardens in Europe.

Mattern, Hermann (1902–71) German landscape architect, an important influence both before and after the second world war. He was Professor of Garden and Landcape Design at Berlin University from 1961.

Persius, Ludwig (1803–45) A German architect, a pupil of Karl Schinkel's, who developed and completed much of Schinkel's work.

Petzold, Eduard Adolf (1815–91) German landscape designer who worked closely with and was influenced by Prince Hermann Pückler-Muskau. His arboretum at Muskau and his numerous textbooks influenced nurseries and nursery management as well as landscape design.

Pückler-Muskau, Prince Hermann von (1785–1871) German landowner and landscape gardener, influenced by Humphry Repton. His own gardens at Muskau and Branitz, his work at Babelsberg and elsewhere, and the *Andeutungen über Landschaftsgärtnerei* (1834) were all important in the development of the 19th-century German landscaping.

Repton, Humphry (1752–1818) English landscape designer, who was the busiest and most influential of his day.

Schinkel, Karl (1781–1841) Important German architect and town planner who was the leading exponent of the neoclassical in Germany.

Schlaun, Johann Conrad (1695–1773) German architect and garden designer who worked at Clemenswerth.

Sckell, Friedrich Ludwig von (1750–1823) German landscape designer, who helped to develop the English landscape style within Germany. He worked at Schwetzingen, the Englischer Garten in Munich, at Nymphenberg, and at Schönbusch.

Index

Acknowledgements

There are many people to thank for their help with this book: my wife Brigid for her involvement at every stage; kind friends and relations who contributed in many ways, including Christopher Blair, John d'Arcy, Walter Erhardt, Mary Keen, Martyn Rix, Patrick Taylor, Christopher Thacker and Basil Williams; the team at Mitchell Beazley, including Guy Croton, Joy Fitzsimmonds, Ruth Hope, Selina Mumford and Anna Nicholas; my agent Barbara Levy for her wise counsels; and above all, the people of Germany, too numerous to list individually, for their invariable courtesy and helpfulness as I researched and visited the gardens in this guide.

Charles Quest-Ritson, *September 1997*

Photographic Acknowledgements

Front jacket: Hugh Palmer
Back jacket: centre, Arcaid/Nic Barlow; bottom, Pictor International; top, Charles Quest-Ritson
Back Flap: Fritz Curzon

All photographs by Charles Quest-Ritson except the following:
AKG, Berlin/Reimer Wulf 15; Patrick Taylor 38, 39, 57, 101